811.52
G31h

69082

DATE DUE			

hawkweed

Books by Paul Goodman

Hawkweed: Poems
Five Years: Thoughts During a Useless Time
The Young Disciple, Faustina, Jonah: Three Plays
Making Do
The Lordly Hudson and Other Poems
Our Visit to Niagara
The Empire City
The Break-Up of Our Camp
Parents' Day
Stop-Light and Other Noh Plays
The Facts of Life

Like a Conquered Province: The Moral Ambiguity of America
People or Personnel: Decentralizing and the Mixed System
Compulsory Mis-Education
The Society I Live In Is Mine
The Community of Scholars
Utopian Essays and Practical Proposals
Growing Up Absurd
Drawing the Line
Communitas (with Percival Goodman)
Gestalt Therapy (with F. S. Perls and Ralph Hefferline)
Art and Social Nature
Kafka's Prayer
The Structure of Literature

⚜ **hawkweed**

poems by Paul Goodman

RANDOM HOUSE NEW YORK

First Printing

© Copyright, 1967, 1966, 1965, 1964, 1963, 1952, 1950, 1947, 1942, by Paul Goodman
All rights reserved under International and Pan-American Copyright Conventions. Published in New York by Random House, Inc., and simultaneously in Toronto, Canada, by Random House of Canada Limited.

Library of Congress Catalog Card Number: 67–22630

Manufactured in the United States of America by H. Wolff Book Manufacturing Co., Inc.
Design by Mary Ahern

The author gratefully acknowledges New Directions for permission to reprint the poems on pages 38-39, 95-96, 150-151, which appeared in *Five Young American Poets* II. Copyright 1941 by New Directions; and the Macmillan Company for the poem on pages 58-70, which appeared in *The Empire City*. © Copyright 1964 by the Macmillan Company. Other poems in the volume originally appeared in: *Poetry*, *Liberation*, *The Massachusetts Review*, *The New York Review of Books*, *Partisan Review*, *The Nation*, *Black Mountain Review*, *i.e. The Cambridge Review* and *Quarterly Review of Literature*.

At evening the dove came back
with a branch of olive in her beak
    and peace after these storms.

NORTH COUNTRY

Sowing, ignorant
of the method—maybe it
will grow anyway.

I slowed the car.
A doe bounded
across the road
and ducking under
the badminton net
went in the woods.
I speeded up.

The Firefly

Mostly I let be, when a snake
is horribly swallowing a frog,
when flocking sparrows peck in anger

3

out the eyes of a murderous kitten,
I take no sides. The nature of things is deadly.
I shudder, but it does not fascinate me
and I go away, not to put a stop.

Yet I have rescued from the octagonal web
of the pinching spider this sick firefly,
I hope in time. I have taken sides.
For late last night this one or one like him
amazed my lonely room with a blue bolt
of lightning, when I was half asleep.

The porch in prudence I repaired last summer
serves me this as the solid state of things
that have been always so.
Evenly gray is the sheen of all the boards
old and new weathered by the winter,
and the post that I made no longer mentions
how the roof was about to fall in ruins.
The backyard is quiet. I have mowed it.
The giant leaves of the red rhubarb spread
their palms out to the sun, and the enormous muzzle
of Henry's cow is munching the bamboo
succulent to her, across my fence.

Our house in the hollow is hemmed in
    also by immense maple trees
but walk a short ways to the meadows
    or up the hills and sky and skies

shatter the world, it cannot hold
    against the gales of openness
whose clouds appear from nowhere
    and drift away southwest.

By the road a small daisy
    stands up among the horizons
a still wheel of eighteen spokes
    and a yellow hub that spins.

It is peaceful coming home across the meadow,
the flowers are continuous as I come.
My bounding beagle somewhere in the hay
is invisible, except her flapping ears
and the white curl of her happy tail
moving through the swaying sea.
The yellow flowers are closing in the evening.
I am not lonely for my only world
is softly singing to me as I come.
They who know me as a bitter critic

who is impractical to serve his country
know me poorly; I am freeborn and pleased
with this world that I have inherited.
And ever my little dog is looking back
with her gleaming eye, and waits if I am coming.

In July the tawny hawkweed
hieracium Canadense
is rioting before the hayer
lays it low, it is on fire
far into the field
where it is peaceful like a world
where there are no human beings.

Sweet as the meadow smells and lovely
as its variety of flowers
was the hour we trudged across the sweet
and various meadow often pausing,
and oh this truthful sentence is
past tense the while I trudge across,
often pausing, the sweet-smelling meadow
lovely with a variety of flowers.

It was good when you were here,
    I am lonely now.
Nighttime is the worst
    when the light drops out of the sky

and the colored fields that were
    company vanish.
I dislike to go out
    into the dark open

but in my empty house
    is the presence of your not-being,
the speech we do not sound,
    the touch I cannot reach.

Surely long ago
    I wrongly set out toward
this familiar encounter
    with no one at all.

During my prime years
    my country passed me by.
I made do. (America
    alas has not made do.)

God bless you who from time to time
    have brought me peace for a day
and saved me from writing only prose
    while my hair turns gray

and may to me God give
    the grace of the poor:
to praise without a grudge
    the facts just as they are.

    ✿

Your ordinary mind, that is the Way.
When you feel sleepy, sleep, et cetera."
It comes to being sleepy, though I still
stagger to the stove to get my dinner.
Three years I made a thousand pages
and a hundred flights across America
and kept an ill-starred love affair alive.
Being alone at last, I droop and drowse.

    ✿

    Clutched in the hot hand
of the child, the flowers wilt
    before we get home.

✣

Brunswick Springs

It isn't Delphi, though it has
sulphurous springs from seven spouts
    and ruins of an hotel
    burned down by the Hoodoo,

yet it is pretty with its pines
and tranquil pond of white lilies
    like the that blind Monet
    painted by telepathy.

It was religious to cleanse
the spa of vandal beer-cans
    as Sally did today
    housewifely for the county.

✣

This tree descends, I guess,
from Johnny Appleseed's seeds
along the valley road
that must have come through here.
The fruit is small, the tree unpruned,
the fruit is sweet, delicious baked,
the tree is like, dotted with red
dots, a piece of jewelry.

September 9, 1964

My birthday was a beautiful day this year
cloudy and blue and the river cool and soft
there were few insects after the cold nights
the corn was ripe and the tomatoes red

the weather held after dark
Jupiter rose among the Pleiades
at midnight, and the sandy road shone
under the dark trees in the starshine.

I love this country whose low hills enclose
my roomy house and serviceable car,
it is here that I choose to be buried
in the far corner of my fertile field.

Here I have assiduously cultivated
being depressed and the bawling inside me
I do not yet know what it is about·
though I have been doing it for fifty years.

Connary, Blodgett, Day, Hapgood
and Dennis are the names in the graveyard
of the abandoned church. The local French

are buried Catholic with their own.
A Jew newcomer, I have also chosen
to lie in this pretty land of my exile.
"Goodman" will look as quiet
as the rest under the maple trees.

Sawyer

These people came up here
only two hundred years ago.
A half a dozen names
of fathers in the graveyard
have brought us to the farmer
who used to be my neighbor.

But now his sons have quit
the beautiful North Country
for Boston where they will not find
a living or even safety.
The boy has joined the Navy
to bomb other farmers
where our Navy ought not to be.

"I set my mind on Richie.
I bought all the machinery for him
and the blue-ribbon cattle.
Now it has no point."
So they have sold and gone

to San Diego
to see the boy on leave.

There will not be another
generation in America,
not as we have known it,
of persons and community
and continuity.
This poetry I write
is like the busy baler
that Sawyer bought for Richie,
what is the use of it?

But I am unwilling to be Virgil
resigned and praise what is no good.
Nor has the President invited me.

Garnered in twenty books
that I count in the barn,
these are the daisies cut
and withered that were beautiful
before the mower passed;
and of the field afire
with hawkweed I extinguished
is neither scent nor glow.

The clover the hawkweed
have burst into bloom
after the hayer
as if summer
could come again,
but the river is cold
and I have eaten
the last raspberry.

EXILE

❧

Long Lines

At 20,000 feet, the earth below was overcast
the flat top of the cloud was like a desert dusted with snow.
At my sunny porthole I agreed to be resigned
as in a bright hospital where they would feed me well
but like one peacefully dying rather than convalescent.
The sky was royal blue to the skim-milky horizon
and the sun was awash in its own golden light,
I stared at hungry with my weeping eyes.
Then were my cares for my sick country quieted
though not forgotten, and the loneliness
in which I ever live was quieted.
Briefly I dimly saw below the wide meandering,
among the Blue Ridge Mountains, Shenandoah River,
and one friendly sparkle from a wave
like a signal to me leaped across four miles of space
saying "God! God!" or "Man! Man!" or "Death!"
or whatever it was, very pleasantly.

Ocean!—

I don't like how I hunger
just for something uncorrupted,
weeping six miles high
just to see idle sparkles
signaling from a river;
inside I must be dying
so frantically to lust for life
above clouds, above eagles.
Indeed, these days my contempt
for the misrulers of my country
is icy and my indignation raucous.
Once American faces
were beautiful to me,
I was their loyal lover,
but now they look cruel
and as if they had narrow thoughts.
Their photographs in *Life*
devastate my soul
as their gasoline denudes
the woods of Indochina.
Let me go into exile
—a poet needs to praise.
It is wicked to live
where I do not care for the people.
What is the use of flailing about
like a wounded animal?
Nothing can come of spite and disdain.

Pilot! please fly on,
do not descend upon my native city.
Ocean!—

Waters and Skies

Waters and skies
hours and seas
are in number plural
before they are singular

and so are gods
joys and sorrows.
But you, my joy
and grief, are singular

like the water from the well
of Bethlehem that David
was thirsty for and other
water was nothing to him,

nor though mankind is my race
can I stay my indignation
at my country's course
as if I had other countries.

Oh I think of leaving here
to go to Crete or Ireland

and what it would be like
to live in a simpler way

but I shall die of my depression
here where I have grown gray,
probably in prison
limited to the last.

Tell me, beautiful,
do any people live
by choices that they make,
or do like me all leap

to the bugle call,
although I just awoke
from a dismaying dream
and the battlefield is a bad one?

But God He is my home
and smiles upon His son
as I write down this poem
in my English tongue.

Commencement, 1962

The insulted poor will riot in my city
without community. The air is poisoned
by crazy sovereigns. America

shamelessly has counterfeited
this ring and book.
                  Thwarted as a man
I grow deluded about my importance
because teen-agers look to me for words.
I am in fact confused like the abandoned
hut in the deep woods with dusty windows
and the town far away, the path grown over with
        blackberry bushes.

Nevertheless! hear the tumultuous west wind
restless in the foliage turning white
that will destroy God knows how much of the world
before retreating he whispers Good-bye
my frightened darlings, thank you.
                     He is whining
and sobbing, he will whistle through his teeth
and howl, and the big branches crack and sag
and wither. I remember Shelley's words,
"Make me thy lyre even as the forest is!"
Something is breathing me despite myself,
my speech is frantic.
                I was too near-sighted
to see the look on the county-leader's face
last night I shouted at him to resign,
and when I called on passers-by on Broadway
"Help! help!" they stood only staring at
each other with impersonal alarm.
Misthrown! I was not meant to be the agent
but the historian of the excellent.

1965

The curses that this peasant spat at us
will torment and destroy us
deadlier than the gasoline
we rained upon her family.

I am afraid to be an American.
Even if we were right, no reason is
so final as the shrieking our marines
have listened to and they will carry home.

We read of things like this in history books
and shudder and get sick. Merciful God,
stop us, our leaders have gone crazy,
listen to them talking like computers.

Where is the little old woman in tennis shoes
        who knew all the annoying facts and figures
and stirred up trouble at the planning-board?
        They humorlessly shot her dead in Georgia.

Up here we used to laugh at her a little
        though she was generally in the right,

she certainly had no head for politics
　　　being only a little old woman in tennis shoes.

Today we smile at the thought of her.
　　　Isn't it strange how we are almost pleased
as we affectionately bring these daisies
　　　to her daughter and her grandchildren?

It must be because she was so old
　　　and soldierly, and in her way quite perfect,
quite perfect, she was in her way quite perfect,
　　　and therefore she is in her way quite perfect.

Washington, D.C.

I am, like Jefferson,
on the axis but across the lagoon.

Surfers at Santa Cruz

They have come by carloads
with Styrofoam surfboards
in the black wetsuits

of the affluent sixties,
the young Americans

kneeling paddle with their palms
and stand through the breakers
One World Polynesians
lying offshore
as if they were fishing for the village.

They are waiting for the ninth wave
when each lone boy falling downhill
ahead of the cresting hundreds of yards
balancing communicates
with the ocean on the Way

how beautiful they are
their youth and human skill
and communion with the nature of things,
how ugly they are
already sleek with narrow eyes.

I grew calm
watching the campfire's
rioting flames

but I am frantic
at the golden prophecy
blinking in the coals:

New Beginning

Loping waltzing marching
happy, quick and proud
and hopping with excitement
we converged on the capital

the bass-drummer beat
and big the brasses blared
our entry was a rout
as if fleeing in disorder

"Peace" was our password
that stung from lip to lip
people spoke in tongues
the future had no shape

we two met in that crowd
that carried us along
I shall not forget the light
of recognition in your eyes

your name is New Beginning
I love you, New Beginning.

SONNETS

Adlai Stevenson

We told the old ambassador to quit:
"These brutal lies you have to tell defame
us and you." "No, I am on the team,"
he said, he was unhappy saying it.
Now he has dropped dead in a London Street
and everyone is weeping over him.
He said, "It's not the way we play the game,
to quit to make a point."
                              The flag is at
half-mast in Springfield. A bombardier reasons
loudly for us in Asia. Our sons
will be commanded to the senseless war
—but many will not go—that does not cease
generation after generation: this
has been no worse but there may not be more.

Flags, 1967

How well they flew together side by side
the Stars and Stripes my red and white and blue
and my Black Flag the sovereignty of no
man or law! They were the flags of pride
and nature and advanced with equal stride
across the age when Jefferson long ago
saluted both and said, "Let Shays' men go!
if you discourage mutiny and riot
what check is there on government?"
                                        Today
the gaudy flag is very grand on earth
and they have sewed on it a golden border,
but I will not salute it. At our rally
I see a small black rag of little worth
and touch it wistfully. Chaos is Order.

A Documentary of Churchill

These images are a remarkable
recapitulation, to again
watch the wars and listen to the men
not making sense, Wilson and Churchill
and Roosevelt, resolute and even noble

in their delusions, until on the screen
victory fades into the next war and vain
policy bursts quietly like a bubble.

What is it with this race that does not learn?
I am weary for meaning and they tire
my soul with great deeds. Yet I cannot turn
my eyes from the stupid story in despair:
since I have undertaken to be born,
Adam, Adam is my one desire.

"We Won't Go"

How many years of history it needed
and stupid choices by how many men
to manufacture this grotesque machine
the sovereign State that yesterday decided
to hurt a simple student who has wanted
little but good in this world and has shown
much good sense although young, my only son
Mathew gentle with animals.
                              Demented
are they, and because we live with them
they drive us mad too, in this beautiful
country they have turned into a slum
with dirty waters and no place where people

are let be, nay they sail across the seas
ten thousand miles to slaughter Vietnamese.

＊

For A. J. Muste and Frank Tannenbaum, 1965

I do not much eulogize dead men,
but when I think of the admirable old
friends that I have, my style that is so cold
and critical otherwise seems to awaken
in generous tribute for our veteran
of peace, A.J., of whom I lately told
the pleasant truth, and lightly I extolled
Frank Tannenbaum touching threescore and ten.

Dismay about my own next years has strained
my voice, and my only world falling apart;
but these old heroes prove they know the art
of living since alive they have remained
(though not without surprises) all of a piece
in the vast wreck of common sense and justice.

For the Committee to Rescue Italian Art

They say the Florentines, that day the Arno
flooded and stormed into Santa Croce
at fifty miles an hour up to three
meters and more, rushed rather to the rescue
of old statues and manuscripts than to
their homes, wives, and children. Naturally,
because these were not things but their city
where climbing on amazing rocks they grew
and thought whatever they thought as they stared
at Perseus lifting the Medusa's head.
There was a moment that the tombs of Machiavelli
and Dante and Galileo Galilei
stood in ten feet of water in the mud
until the water started to recede.

O'Hare Airport

For wearing out the spirit with dull size
O'Hare's the worst, it is a fitting gate
to come into Chicago, if your feet

still drag their shoes and if your weary eyes
survive the miles of Stygian blue. Be wise,
lovers of light and wit and you sedate
humanists, tribe of Erasmus, to evade
this labyrinth upon your winged ways.
Our number is grown few, our patience
these days is frayed; though we are sweet and bland
by disposition, we are known to kill
or die of grief meeting the imbecile.
And through these corridors they pipe a canned
music that is neither song nor dance.

Freud

First through blooming fields of hell among
colored dreams, gay jokes, and gorgeous
mistakes our guide had conducted us
to where desire, the dragon of my song,
was flaming in his nether parts and tongue.
Next we were exploring hideous
wastes of heaven by salt pools of loss,
and spiny cactuses of right and wrong,
even to the Sphinx the wish for death
—and here we stood awhile to catch our breath

when suddenly dead for all our hopes and fears
is our guide across the sky and deep,
this morning a surprise of bitter tears,
a friendly dream now that I am asleep.

For My Sister

Of us three who fifty years and more
have worked too hard, Alice has always been
unassertively a kind of captain
of our attentive course, she, noted for
kindness. Now age is driving us ashore
toward death's rocks and our sister is again
the first among us, to be gravely stricken
and guide us nowhere.
                    But outside the door
of the infirmary the nurse tells us,
"Oh she's a tough old bird and she'll pull through."
The corridor is crowded with her friends
astounded she is ill, who never was;
she told them not to let her brothers know
so we would not be bothered while she mends.

Transfigured both the fucked and the fucker's face
beyond beautiful—terrible, austere,
more alike than people otherwise appear
as every breath draws nearer the animal race
drowning in uproar, as in the witch-grass
of Easter Island the strange heads uprear,
preclassical with lips like a nightmare
high up the hillside in that lonely place

how came they there? to our surprise
as our new ship approaches in the sunrise.

The ocean is around a thousand miles,
the noisy surf is battering the gunwale,
the stones are not wearing human smiles,
the sculptors did not speak a known tongue.

For Taylor

Taylor, these unreasonable days
gentle it is how we have been for each

other practical and often sweet
friends. I am not bashful to praise
how we in spite of persons and bad laws
and the envious opinion of the street
enjoy our simple sex without deceit
that others fear and hide for no good cause.

Exactly of a continent the span
divides us now: you where upon the rocks
the seals play outside the Golden Gate,
I watch the stormier Atlantic that
ceaselessly on Fire Island knocks,
who only yesterday were hand in hand.

Almost everything lovely in my eyes
is banned to me by law or circumstance
or impractical people. Sometimes a long chance
and hard labor have given me a prize
but grace ought to be easy, the surprise
when need is met halfway in its advance.
Fighting to wrest my inheritance
I have stayed alive not in paradise,
I am not cheerful, I who always taught
others to intelligently beguile
gloomy bogey-men am myself caught

in mid-career with a freezing smile.
I look at common daylight as a waste
and at the streets around me with distaste.

March April May June

The March loves that Braggadocio
is boasting about so won't live till spring,
it's sleeting outside and that whistling
gale is not blowing here from Mexico.
But the friendship under seven feet of snow
that we two husbandmen are nourishing
prudent of seasons and diffidently holding
hands for warmth until the morning
                                        oh!
I'll wheel my motorcycle from the hall
into April, and we two cruise behind
our flapping banner in a southern wind
into May, and dogwood will again
stun to anguish my defeated soul
alone among the meadowflowers in June.

For My Birthday, 1956

Mars is near this month, whatever that means.
To me he looks not baleful but inquiring
peach-colored in the west. When we go soaring
yonder weightless, as I fly in dreams,
the tired earth will fall away betimes
and new and promising to our admiring
another shore will open for exploring,
that planet that in my reflector shines.

This project makes me proud and picks me up
and buoys me up with a patient hope.

But friends, who ask me what I want or need
on my birthday, teach me fortitude
to face the illness that has struck my daughter
who was like me full of knowing laughter.

Schumann's Violin Concerto

Music and speechless death in league
perfect and kill. Times they go wrong
—a poor musician ages, Keats died young—
but mostly, as if fearing to fatigue,

Music gives up her favorite: once big
and now delivered, no soul overlong
is able to live. Tchaikovski wrote a song
of adequate gloom and died; the little jig
at a big question was for Beethoven
what he had to say to us; and when
he scratched these repetitions, Schumann came
to the madhouse and death. I therefore watch
my poems morbidly for the one in which
I finally shall recognize my name.

The age of life I am, Beethoven died
unhappier than I and lonelier
than human beings ought to let each other.
He had when he took death for a bride
never known another. Rough and rude
he came in character an awkward lover,
yet she did not rebuff him nor defer
the night.
          Myself, I have often cried
when he speaks to me. Everything is plain
between us, definite and understood,
but what to do with it I cannot guess.
Many hours we have spent we twain
conversing; what he says is very good
but when he leaves off I am at a loss.

On the Sonnet

These hand-me-downs of Milton that I wear
I wear well, we are a family
baroque, ambitious for too rich a joy,
except that we are duteous and severe.
The fourteen verses of the sonneteer
are thoughtful about this anomaly
but in spite of us the passionate outcry
interrupts.
        Things being what they are,
mostly we are indignant as we write,
God did not make the world to be the best
but man has monstrously insulted it.
At other times more gently we have witnessed
(as if surprised) the being of some sweet
friend like you, David, in the waste.

BALLADS AND STORIES

Ballad of the Pentagon

Staughton Lynd he said
      to the Secretary of War,
"If on my little son
      this can of gasoline I pour,

"can you light a match to him?
      do you dare?"
The master of the Pentagon
      said nothing but sat there.

"Then how do you command
      your soldiers to rain
blazing gasoline
      on little yellow children?"

This happened in America
      in 1965
that people talked about
      burning children alive.

Now Norman Morrison
      heard this conversation

and he took his stand in front of
        the frowning Pentagon.

He had his baby in his arms
        but in his mind I know not what
for he also said nothing
        except to whisper to the tot:

"Let me show you all the things,
        baby whom I adore,
this is the United States
        and here sits the Secretary of War.

"Here is the broad blue sky
        with the sun at my right hand,
and far far far down there
        are people and the sea and land."

He poured the gasoline upon
        himself and the baby
but when he lit the human torch
        he threw the baby out of harm's way.

How long can this continue,
        how long can this go on,
these crazy incidents
        in front of the Pentagon?

My country falling to pieces
        —these frantic demonstrations—
jumping up and down
        with signs in frustration—

—Our public men machines—
    Norman Morrison
afire with determination
    in front of the Pentagon.

    ☥

Ballad of the Truck by the River

Ah cain't afford to get a hard-on, boss,
    cause it cost a nigger money to screw
an ah cain't make a livin in dis town
    count o dis yere Jim Crow.

So ah sits here out o mischief in de sun
    singin an meditatin dis an dat
an jes' avoidin any lil fancy
    as is liable to get my nuts hot.

But if yo wanna fuck me, sho,
    ah likes to feel a white man's push
as got a job an ain't ascairt
    to dirty yo pants cause you can wash.

To make me feel dat ah belong
    white man's cock is better'n pot
an it usually don't cos' nuthin
    which usually is what ah got.

De river's bright today, ain't it?
    it's hot in de back o dis yere truck.
Jes' shove it in. Ah recollec'
    when ah was a kid ah had a cock.

My mammy when her knees was spread
    an she was solid wi' dat man
she said she was at rest in Jesus
    like a turnip in de groun'.

An when yo push it in an out
    boss boss o New York town,
ah jes' so happy an belongin
    like dat turnip in de groun'.

Lyin yere grinnin and watchin de river
    fo company while ah gets fuck
is jes' like home where ah was born,
    some niggers dey got all de luck.

A Man from Georgia

As to this dirty broken man from Georgia
weeping and with a bandaged head, I gave
my pipe to smoke and thirty cents for breakfast,
neighborly words without disdain, but not
a bath nor clothing nor a ticket home
nor useful information—so myself

in need I get thirty cents of affection,
thus much I have in me to give and get.

I saw him later, washed and not too bad
but drunk on apple-wine. "Hey, I know you,
you're the good guy," he said, "the one New Yorker
ever give me a nickel. Thanks a lot, suh.
Have a drink." I drank it without grace
to be polite. I am the more confused
about the nature of things and my own role.
I could not shake him off all afternoon.

Bitterly he told me how three niggers
had knocked him down and took ten dollars off him.
No doubt they did, no doubt he provoked them.
"I thought," he said, "when I come to New York
I'll be a big shot. Lying there like that
like a shitty tramp. They left me in the gutter
to die," he whined, "bleedin." I remained
impassive, cheerful, optimistic.

I know that life is simple. It is hard
but simple. Living is not complicated,
but it is very hard and very simple.
I don't think anyone would say that living
is easy, though to some (I can imagine)
living which is to me horribly hard
is just that easy, but they wouldn't say so,
people like that wouldn't say anything.

Ballad of Jenny and the Firemen

When all that's left is dirty glasses
    and the butts are cold upon the floor
is a melancholy moment, chum,
    but it's worse if the party is next door.

When she went to complain about the din
    she caught them necking in the hall
but nobody invited her in.
    Drinking alone is worse than none at all.

But how do you bear the unearthly silence
    when the last laugh is swallowed in the gloom?
Did they all leave? Maybe Roberts
    is stretched out dead in the bathroom.

She's got to scream, she can't help it
    —splits your ears a scream like that,
it pins you cold sober
    echoing in the night.

"I'll turn in a fire alarm!"
    —that's a happy notion!
"I'll have a lot of company
    in the hullaballoo and commotion.

"Firemen are gentlemen,
        they smash the furniture professionally,
not like drunken bums." She giggles
        at such a vigorous idea.

Softly shines the orange globe
        of the firebox on Eighty-first
where the park is closed after dark
        because of muggers and perverts.

It's mysterious at 3 A.M.
        under the lamp on the corner of the street
while Jenny waits for the engingines
        to come in about a minute.

The residential neighborhood is quiet.
        The siren sounds far away.
There's time to light a cigarette
        while a beagle lifts his leg to pee.

(Between the act and its effect
        I fell into a revery
that I could never recollect
        when the loud clang awakened me.)

"Where's the fire?" "This way, men!"
        She leads the huskies with the pole and axe
graciously to her apartment
        where beer is in the icebox.

The hook-and-ladder fills the block.
        Sleepy people look out the windows.

The chief arrives in his red coupé.
    The firemen unroll the hose.

They smash the furniture. "Hey, what goes on?"
    cries Roberts, rushing to the scene
without shoes. "No!" says Jenny,
    "*that* one is drunk, don't let *him* in."

Five firemen with rubber coats
    can crowd a spacious living room.
Their ways are rough, their muddy boots
    are like the peony in bloom.

🜪

A Hustler

No, Ronny, sit and talk.
Let's skip the sex. I'll buy your beer.
What good are your muscular arms
if you won't hold onto me?
I see your cock is hard
but you'll lie there like a lamp post."

Yet he was not ridiculous.
He kept his glum green eyes averted.
They looked at me dartingly.
His forehead was perplexed.

His solid frame was mute
but had a mute appeal that was alive.
He didn't want to go away. I said:
"Try to say it. What are you thinking of?
I'll find you words." I guessed that he would bawl
if father treated him gentle for a change.

He said, "I'm not thinkin about anythin.
Ast me a question so I have somethin to say.
Mostly when I sit like this I am
not thinkin about anythin at all.
Maybe I'm thinkin about so many things
I dunno what I'm thinkin about, it's sub
conscious, maybe."
                "Don't you ever cry,"
His eyes were scalding hot; connecting sentences
opened the abyss of making sense
which he could ill afford. "Naw, I don't cry."
"What's bad about crying?" "Nothin's bad,
only you ast me, no, I never cry."
"Don't you feel like crying now, Ronny?"
"Naw, I don't feel it," Ronny said and wept
—one tear and panicked. "Why do you bother?
why is everybody innerested in *me?*
I'm just one o the fellers."
                    The conceit
shone brilliantly out of his sidelong leer,
he waited baited for a compliment,
his long hair was combed Puerto Rican style.

"Suppose you could, what would you like to do?"
"You'll laugh at me," he said. "No, I won't laugh."

"I'd like to be an actor." "Marlon Brando?"
"I don' need to imitate Marlon Brando,"
he said indignantly, "I'll act myself!"
"Why don't you?" "I am waitin to be discovered."

☩

The Ballad of St. Patrick

I tell St. Patrick about the condition of Ireland

Patrick, it's a sad story
    of the emerald isle in the West
depopulated by the plotting
    of your thin-lipped priest

and Greedy Witch the Irish mother,
    these two have made a blight,
although from Cork to Donegal
    the daffodils are bright.

Says Thin Lips, "If a lad and lass
    go walking, it's a mortal sin,
they'll burn in hell for it," he gloats
    and oh his lips are thin.

And Greedy screeches, "Shame on you,
    ungrateful whore, your filthy tricks!

Stay home and take care of your mother,
　　time enough when you're thirty-six."

Was it for this you set ablaze
　　the bonfire on Tara
and shamrock spread where'er you trod
　　from Meath to Connemara?

From Glendalough to Connemara
　　the lakes of Ireland are blue
yet what can a lively fellow do
　　but skulk in a pub and stew

and brag of what he would do
　　if he ever did anything,
and old men reminisce about nothing
　　on a scratchy string?

Till the roaring rage of it all,
　　how the lustless spring is sped,
catches them by the throat
　　and some of them break each other's head,

but most become resigned
　　and passionately then
they wager on lovely horses
　　ridden by other men.

The Saint tells how he rested from his labors

Mea culpa! Patrick moans,
     I meant it for the best.
I was a fool old and blind.
     He smites on his embroidered breast.

I labored to introduce a little
     learning and civility
—little I had—the manners
     of Rome across the sea

to dirty barbarian pirates
     that kidnaped me as a boy,
repaying like a Christian
     love for injury with joy.

(And pride and joy I've had to praise
     John Scot's mind and Tom Moore's voice,
and bitterness when Dublin brays
     at John Synge and Jamie Joyce.)

With a gentle winning nature
     and wrath only for cruelty
I brought peace to that brawling race
     and I was satisfied with me.

I built a house in Armagh
     for the gifts I got in Rome
and there I rested my worn-out eyes
     waiting to go home.

The fire of the Resurrection
    on Tara blazed and in Kildare
the fire of fertile Brigit,
    now wasn't that a grand pair!

The Saint falls a prey to the ever watchful Devil

Woe! and you'll laugh when you hear
    —no laughing matter—how poor old Pat
did a disservice to Ireland
    and fell in the Devil's trap.

Arrogance was my vice,
    it drove a saint to make mistakes:
"I'll build an earthly paradise,"
    I said, "and ban the snakes!"

The innocent snakes that slither
    in black holes out of the sun
with as much right as us to bite
    whatever interferes with fun,
the old fool swore with a great furor
    he'd root out every one.

"Ha ha!" howled the Adversary
    and he bounded out of Chaos
—God bless him, he keeps us wary—
    "The snakes is it? my arse!

"old Pat is blind as a bat
    he wouldn't know the difference

between a you-know-what
and a snake or other indecence.

"I'll make up as his deacon
and help him on his rounds."
God save me! groaned St. Patrick,
I banished out of bounds

every young lively cock
in Ireland from that black
Friday in 457
until of Doom the crack!

*St. Patrick and the Devil prepare to ban the snakes
from Ireland*

Lad, help me with my amice and alb.
That Devil tucked me in.
When he touched my pectoral cross
I did not see him turning green.

My chasuble of lace and jewel
I labored under like a horse,
I was a fat and pompous fool,
he pushed my mitre on my nose.

Give me my crozier in my hand
that knocked the idol of Cromm Cruach down
in County Cavan! said I grand,
Pig-ears the cowboy on the town.

And look ye, bring the magic book
        that has the words and no mistakes.
Rat-a-tat-tat! here comes Pat!
        where are these Irish snakes?

"Your Grace looks like a million dollars,"
        he flattered me, "that damnèd brood
will hang their tails between their legs,
        so to speak, when we say the word.

"Ah, here is the form: *Every worm
        over five inches, make it six,
that lifts its head and starts to squirm
        and especially if it spits,*

"*Come out into the April sun!
        one fond farewell and begone!
retire underground
        or quit this island on the run!*"

So armed with staff and words
        we came into the Irish spring,
the fishes were leaping in Lough Neagh,
        the swallows darting on the wing,

the dandelions in the grass
        a-riot. And every rosy cock
was also snuffling the air
        as by we came with bell and book.

It never used to rain so much,
        aye, and the sun was closer to us

63

those days we smiled on growing things
and we let nature take her course.

*Tricked by the Devil, the Saint makes a disastrous
mistake*

Sang out that damnèd spirit, "Look!
    here rears a monstrous serpent. You!
reveal yourself to Father Pat!
    a foot long, give an inch or two."

It was an Irish fisherboy
    holding his patient line
and thoughtfully playing with himself
    in the hot sunshine.

With blushing pride the innocent youth
    took it out for show,
glad for God and the public world
    his bravery to know.

His prick looked up with dumb inquiry
    like a puppy to be petted, oh
I could not see the charming sight.
    "Go!" cried I, "monstrous serpent, go!

"quit the sod of Ireland!
    no longer tempt Mother Eve!"
I said it like a Jesuit,
    who would have believe?

because I never found, not I,
    when I was young and incontinent,
that my reservoir ran dry
    or it kept me from becoming a saint

—the contrary! the more you come
    the more you can. Period.
Attend to lowly things, my lad,
    and you'll attain the glory of God.

The blind Saint makes another mistake

Now that Devil ran ahead of me
    disguised in a low-cut gown
and a wriggle of the behind
    but never the tail shown,

to entice a simple cowboy
    lying dreaming on the lawn
(he was a damned entrapper
    like cops in a California town),

and when in hope the lad stood up
    and his moist eyes were a benison
for this lovely saint from heaven sent,
    the entrapper shouted, "Another one!

"Pat, grab it!" "Ouch!" I cried, "this one
    is hot as blazes and hard as wood.
Lord, Lord! who ever heard
    of a rigid reptile with warm blood?"

"Those are the worst! here is the book:
  Hot-blooded snakes, they prowl by night
and day and accost young ladies
  or anybody else in sight.

"*Of these the so-called rigid species*
  has an indiscriminate appetite,
be wary of him, he is hard
  and hungry and about to bite."

"Be banished!" I release my grip
  in horror of the risk I run.
"O father," says the boy, "a minute more
  I would have got my gun."

  And many many more mistakes

"For heaven's sake! a Jewish snake
  with a big nose I see!"
"Suppressed, suppressed like all the rest!
  Ireland sober is Ireland free!"

Ireland sober is Ireland free—
  did y' ever hear such idiocy?
Ireland free is Ireland sober,
  Ireland free o' the likes of me!

A well-assorted pair we were
  who walked through Ireland on April First,
I scattered blessings on every hand
  and everything I blessed I cursed,

I and my entrapper,
    a devil with a false book
and a fat fool with a mitre
    abusing his shepherd's crook.

Oh and the pitiful result
    of my misguided enterprise
is a million copies of Shawn Keough
    holding their fists in front o' their flies.

The length and breadth of Ireland
    fine women keened, their hair they tore
as rat-a-tat-tat there went Pat
    from Parknasilla to Bangor,

old Pat blind as a bat
    from County Down to County Clare,
never got my sandals wet
    so the Aran Islands are still there.

"The fire of fertile Brigit
    is going out!" the women keened,
but I paid no mind as I inclined
    to the dogma of the Fiend.

*Only the Laughing Laddy of Lough Neagh escapes
the curse*

One likely laddy and one alone,
    whose name I dare not tell

(for the government of Ireland
   is still a fief of hell)

escaped because he loved me:
   he figured, "That's not Pat
led like a bear by the nose
   under that ridiculous hat.

"Pat reads the book himself
   not far from common sense.
Now my sex is as neat as the next
   but this is no time for romance;

"in the wildwood and with madmen
   trust the wisdom of your toes."
With a last laugh into Lough Neagh
   he deftly dove and the bubbles rose.

And there he waits immortal
   for truth and nature never wane,
he sticks his head up every morning
   to see if the people are yet sane.

That laughing Laddy of Lough Neagh
   has a head on his shoulders broad
instead of a block, and a rosy cock
   that he'll protect by force or fraud,

O Laddy of Lough Neagh, would
   that I could call, Come out! begin!
begin the reign of sense again!
   purge St. Patrick of his sin!

Darling! take your Irish bride!
    Nay, as it is, Stay in! stay in!

Saint Pat is standing on the shore
    and tears are flowing down my beard,
my longing arms are stretched toward hope—
    Lord, must not such a prayer be heard?

The Moral of it all is that First Things are First

Well, whether I drave the snakes away
    I do not know, I doubt it,
but this I know, our boys are slow
    and in a pinch they do without it.

Seamas cowers when Mama lowers
    and hides his penis between his legs,
while Timothy goes over the sea
    leaving Ireland to the bogs.

And isn't it a shame? I love
    their freckles and their brogue and blarney,
their speech is lilting music still
    and even their jokes are pretty funny,

but there is no use or future
    of a lad won't take his penis out
or when he does can't get it up
    or if he gets it up can't shoot.

The fire of fertile Brigit
    is going out: there's a thought
to freeze your testicles but good!
    Forbid it, God! Man, look to't!

For to have lovely children
    takes patience, intellect, and luck,
and God's grace, and affection,
    but first you have to f.

Adult Education, 1935

Now let me teach this Dialogue,
    the little hand is touching eight
—my throat is tickled by the fog—
    the man from Newark will come late,

neatly pull his rubbers off,
    and sit down next to Mrs. Brooks.
By way of starting I will cough.
    Do all the desks have open books?

And what will Plato do for us,
    for Mrs. Kraus whose heart is weak
and therefore she is studious,
    for Troy who cycles like a streak

because his soul is ill at ease?
    What if tonight I did not break
the Great Books Tuesday Evening peace
    but listened to the ticking clock?

No, I'll speak out soon enough
    —I often am in doubt this way—
once I start, once I cough,
    I lose myself in what I say.

The mole that Dr. Davidson
    above his golden eyebrow wears
is what I'll fix my eyes upon
    and hear my voice go down the stairs.

And what will it be like when I
    have said what Proclus said he said?
The ancient learning will not die,
    young Blake will toss upon his bed

with longing for the Upward Way
    among other fantasies of sex,
Miss Simkovich will learn to say
    the while her father's business wrecks,

"The soul departs before the body,"
    and when the khaki sentry tires
and drops to his knees, McGillicuddy
    will close his eyes before he fires.

1934: A Train Wreck at Sixty-sixth Street

The iron El stood overhead.
Bronze Dante like a man of God
in the green triangle stood.
"Listen," thought I to the crowd
milling about,
"he wants to speak—" but the railroad
was growling and my thought
I could not yet speak out.

A pigeon on his copper head
sprang and sank therein his feet.
A living silence spread.
"Look," I whispered without breath
to the deaf,
"the metal man is quiet
in this clamor of death
like Ser Brunetto's shade
in the whirlwinds and the heat."

Snorting sparks, the train came forward.
Dante like a sword
raised his arm without a word
and the dragon cowered
and hid his light behind his shoulder;
he clambered down on haunches awkward
and crouched where Dante petted his deep-scarred

forehead gently. I stood proud,
I have had my reward.

Ballad of the Coral Bar

He was a beautiful mechanic
    till his wife cut him down to size,
now he walks the street and haunts
    the Coral Bar with yellow eyes.

His rosy cock was quick to rise
    and he was one to have his way,
she did not move, she did not moan,
    she turned her stony face away

She patiently did nothing
    while he jumped up and down,
and so the dead defeat the living
    in the long run.

Twice a week for fifteen years
    adds up to fifteen hundred tries
(the measure is Martin Luther's)
    —she cut them all down to size.

"Wife, you have won the game,
    to play games I did not marry.
But don't expect me to forgive
    your hard-bought victory."

He tried no more. She took a lover
    who flattered her a Friday night
and she was happy as a fool
    and had the fulness of delight.

For it is easier to love
    a lover than your daily mate,
and some of it, I guess, is fear,
    and some is nothing but spite.

There are no kids to interrupt
    when you fuck with your lover
and you can feed on fantasies
    like a cow in clover.

"Husband," she taunted, "how is this?
    I have delight I never had."
They will do it every time,
    insult to injury to add.

"Full fifteen years," she wept, "I lost
    the best years of my youth!"
She said no more for with his paw
    he slapped her on the mouth,

he threw in her disdainful teeth
    the years of insult to his hard-on,

the lovely gift he used to offer
        as if begging her pardon.

Making of the strength he had
        this miserable use
he left her lying on the floor
        bleeding from the eyes and nose.

Farewell to glory! to the wheels
        farewell, that were towed in
and out they rolled upon their own
        while he watched with a grin.

Farewell to courage! to the penis
        that rose ten thousand times again,
but New York City gives no medals
        to such a citizen.

Lover! rescue her you likened
        to the Venus of the Medicis,
but you have gone away, I hear,
        to Los Angeles.

This is a tale I heard or told
        Saturday in the Coral Bar,
I cannot remember which it was
        but it rang familiar.

Epode. The New Bus Terminal

I thought, "Why, I'll go in and see this new
this marvel where the buses overhead
roar to the provinces. It's not all finished
but through the rags I'll see the flesh the better
like this lad with a rip in his pants—"
A mason's boy was polishing the cornerstone
and I admired the progress of his work,
but he was busy.
            So I came inside
out of the lousy season dignified
on calendars as our first month. And why
am *I* freezing in this Hanseatic town
fit for fur hats, and I am no merchant,
when that bus is bounding over the viaduct
southward to Key West?
            To my surprise
I was enchanted. Gleaming escalators
were elevating travelers through the ceiling.
Everything was shining and in motion.
The chromium handrailing took a thumbprint.
Then I was standing on the mezzanine
lordly overlooking the Grand Concourse
where I could window shop the passersby
—with one eye on the prowling cop—and smoke
my pensive pipe in peace.
            Glory to God!
rough-scored with plaster like the Milky Way

came by that mason's boy; he looked at me,
our glances met, he smirked—as thirds at last
in the A-Minor Adagio of Haydn
fill out the wide skip in the melody
and this arpeggio is the climax,
he frowned self-consciously. I followed hard.

God damn the labyrinth that we have built!
laid for us—by us—we become confused—
I lost him in an unknown corridor,
inside my soul and on Fortieth Street.
There is no reason to an American plan,
we are leased out to shops, we dig in subways,
the ancient simplicity is gone!
Gone is the interesting from this house!
That chromium was tarnished long ago.
Those buses leap to no good south and west,
black care drives with the driver as he drives.
How did I give this stupid Terminal
even my provisional assent?
Yet let me praise the star-eyed mason's boy
who meant as much as I did to make sense.

Bread and Wine

An empty container that cannot be filled is nothing
     at all.
     Smash you! *be* nothing.

My hope is no longer hollow
    ow! I am no longer disappointed.

The shards do not reproach me as violent,
    each broken piece has a bright outline.
I love you, immortal contents of the smashed
    empty container that could not be filled.

I am immortal drunken on the raw
    draught of my no longer disappointment.

Who is this tipsy fellow who is dancing,
    dancing for joy as though he were in love?

He has drunken the immortal contents
    of an empty container that could not be filled.

He smashed it on a rock. There on the ground
    the broken shards have each a bright outline.

He keeps repeating how he broke the jug.

I too feed daily on the non-being of Paradise
    of which a month ago I gave up hope.

So I have put on needed weight
    and people remark that I look younger.

I was distraught with longing for Paradise
    convinced that it was unattainable for me.

I came to my senses about Paradise
　　　at 142 West 23rd Street
　　　which building now is down
　　　and there is a parking lot.

Such is my bread and wine. Creator Spirit,
　　　let me make a song too, like Yuan Ming
　　　on his lute that had no strings, he was so poor.

MAKING LOVE

For M.H.

Your face your profile while we fuck
is not from heaven, it does not float,
is like the big pale-golden
pebble I picked up
from a Smoky Mountain freshet
ground by the torrents of the spring
and polished by warm sparkling waters
millions of summer afternoons
until this norm of rural granite

—I showed it to the artist-students
laboriously molding abstract shapes:
"No use," I said. "These native stones
are the refinement of enormous powers
applied a billion semesters
millions of storms and still in the making,
you cannot match it! try at something else—"

Say out you love me, tell me any lies
in order that in order that
closely blotted to you I may wander
somewhere, anywhere, and lose my wits.
Someone once said to me,

"You have a human face
lined with experience." I was embarrassed.

†
♣

We had a few moments of quiet beauty
in our dark room lit by lamplight through the trees.
They were not in the reliable order of events
nor in the practical order of what I know to do.
I did not know what to do with this
—too close, inside arm's length, to ward it off—
only to murmur "Stay! O thou! last long!"
but I grew uncomfortable in the unbearable
pauses sweet in which I could not rest
and soon lapsed into lust and fell asleep.

Those beautiful moments we deserved who tried,
we tried hard, both daring and forbearing,
to preserve the possible into a fact.
Honor and good judgment guarded us
like angels. We were proud of being lucky.

Oh, even while I lay there at a loss
how to cope with this closer than opportunity,
I was in a panic for the shameful waste
—badly nourished by my only world
I am alive to the sin of waste!

And now these things have left me as I am.
As I did not know what to do with that

I cannot find myself in the world as it is.
I am distraught with longing for paradise,
convinced it is unattainable for me.

Haverford

Never did I see so much lovely dogwood
tamed on lawns as yesterday at Haverford
both pink and white, and also Peter Bevin
proud of his pitching and very wide his grin
like the youngster's on the cornflakes box.
To meet "a real writer who wrote books"
he sought me out.
                    He was a troubled boy
late last night among his friends when I
long hours leveled my attention at him,
at only him. And all the time
we kept looking into each other's eyes,
not catching each other at it by surprise
but as if endlessly drinking, in spite of
himself in love, I willingly in love.

"He for God Only, She for God in Him"

"Thank you, it was sweet. My ready wits
are like myself again. I can forget
how we just lay body along body
and I drunken breathing in your breath
—now for this General Motors Corporation
that makes my town unlivable, and this
Federal Bureau of Investigation
that makes my country coward! oh today
I'll bring low these insolent giraffes!"
So boasts he, while the white sun blazes
full on his forehead in the fresh outdoors.
She with pride and hope watches him vanish,
still feeling fucked, soon dreamily intent
on his seed in her belly quietly.

Gene, John, Jojoy, Jerry,
Lor, and Hal were lovers I had
and all we were rarely merry,
sometimes we were sad.

Trusting, we were not betrayed,
shrewdly enough we sought our chances;

mathematically unmade
we were, by times and distances.

But now the circumstance and duty
that hurried us and harried us
are no more, but abide the beauty
and attentiveness that married us.

Oh the beauty and the madness and the strangeness
of my six lovers astonishes me
as I murmur their names I used to say
aloud on better mornings than today.

Joan Cowan

I somehow learned with grander thrusts
     and joy to make love and fearless feeling
—as I never could with Joan Cowan—
     those hours that I watched appealing
the radiant smile of Joan Cowan.

Another fills and fills it well
     of both my arms the warm embrace
—as they never were full of Joan Cowan—
     never felt but an empty ache
for the body of Joan Cowan.

At the contour of a lovely song
        I weep hot tears for my thwarted past
—as I wept them for Joan Cowan—
        but they'll be wept away at last
and I'll think with thanks of Joan Cowan.

※

Lines

His cock is big and red when I am there
and his persistent lips are like sweet wine.
Then would I pause and breathe his closeness
a long time hungrily, for it is there.
Yet we dress in haste and friendly say good-bye
and do not intend, each for our own good reasons,
to commit ourselves to happiness together.
Our meetings are fortunate and beautiful,
he is chaste and I am temperate,
for I have learned by the unlikely way
of deficiency and excess temperance.

※

A Little Epithalamion for a Wedding at Our School

Dragging its feet the spring
across the ragged grass

is April like a flash
and thick as thoughts the sparrows wing
into the sunrise of
Amy and Lew in love.

Now loosed the streams like incorrigible girls
meander where they must not go
and like bad boys the gales blow
across the world in swirls
this wayward morning of
Amy and Lew in love.

In the original colors lit
in Paradise to heat man's soul
the flowers of the field are slowl-
y burning to nothing bit by bit
through the long midday of
Amy and Lew in love.

With one paw raised and bared his teeth
my dog is arrested by the hush
of dusk, and in the whispering brush
the hare has vanished like a breath.
Sudden is the evening of
Amy and Lew in love.

Night speaks not. From pole to pole
the Milky Way flows motionless
and every star without distress
exists and all together roll,
the speechless midnight of
Amy and Lew in love.

"We Have a Crazy Love Affair"

We have a crazy love affair,
it is wanting each other to be happy.
Since nobody else cares for that
we try to see to it ourselves.

Since everybody knows that sex
is part of love, we make love;
when that's over, we return
to shrewdly plotting the other's advantage.

Today you gazed at me, that spell
is like why I choose to live on.
God bless you who remind me simply
of the earth and sky and Adam.

I think of such things more than most
but you remind me simply. Man,
you make me proud to be a workman
of the Six Days, practical.

At Stanford

John said (he cared for me),
"Now get some sun, take it easy.

But no, you'll overwork as usual,
I'll get the sun before you will."
He was wrong, he fell in a rage
and they have put him in a cage,
while I lie here by the lagoon
with my shirt off in the sun
at Stanford College in the west.
My sexless spirit knows no rest
thinking of John who cared for me
and told me to take it easy.

Animal Spirits

Sometimes since you don't love me any more
    I cannot find an animal spirit
    to move my feet,
    or one quits and leaves me in the street
among the buses and the traffic's roar

as if I were deep in thought, but I am not
    —until the animal spirit that preserves
    me still alive
    takes care of where I am and slowly drives
my feet their way across the street.

What have I lost, having lost your love?
        Very little, very little.
        Busy with your private riddle
you did not have much love to give.
                Always you were impractical
                and came late or not at all.

I have lost caring for you hurt,
        long days of dread for you,
and many guilty thoughts that
        my influence was bad for you,
                but I was frank with you! to whom
                now I shall not show this poem.

If I begin tonight to cry
        I shall not soon stop crying.
Every day that passes by
        I am nearer dying.
                You cared for that, why I know not,
                but having lost your love I've lost it.

May

My darling Sally is
        and what for me in April

she did was amiable,
maybe May will more than this

open to me her heart
        to my delight to my
        wandering wonder my
lost onward steps and newfound art.

Then Persephone
        the queen of hell and flowers
        will idly guide my course
to where is guessed, not known, by me.

My hands are shuddering
        but I am not afraid
        for it is I who made
Alcestis and *The Dead of Spring*.

In George's Tavern

For God's sake, sailor, I'd be glad
to suck your eager cock off
but what you say about Negroes
makes my hair crawl; you're stupid
and stupidity is graceless.
Cupid died when you opened your mouth.

Oh if they wouldn't open their mouths,
the beauties whose roses grow
in a tropical garden, and God
wove them from wild stuff
—if they wouldn't open their mouths!

To Eros praise! who by unreason
binds us to humanity
with marines, the butchers of their brothers.
We close our ears and stomach horror,
and lust unpardoning.

Ballade of Difficult Arrangements

He's drunk again and doesn't show,
my wife is home he can't come here,
yesterday the bus was slow;
or let's suppose the coast is clear,
deep in slumber lies my dear.
We have our moments even so
and fuck and fondle front and rear,
but happiness is touch and go.

Even though neither one says No,
to get both bodies to appear
has been a science I don't know,

though I a yellow hood can wear
and slashes blue in sleeves that flare.
Yet times we kiss and times we blow
and other times we just sit near,
but happiness is touch and go.

He's off to work, money's low,
my wife is lonely, I love her,
he keeps on terms with Tom and Joe,
at dinner I'm in Daddy's chair;
how can you be both here and there?
Nevertheless we whisper slow
sweet talk in each other's ear,
but happiness is touch and go.

Mercury, bring the distant near!
Apollo, make the sun go slow!
Linger longer, fleeting year!
Happiness is touch and go.

Ballade for Jean Cocteau

Martyrs of the crimes of sex,
Sappho, Hyacinth, and she
who fucked the Bull, and Oedipus Rex,
they are not by Jean and me

blotted out of memory
but wept and named, so all may read
and know them and ourselves and ye.
But to heaven was raped Ganymede.

Read, all, and pay respects
of etiquette to outlawry;
don't look away, fate protects
these names from shame: Pasiphaë
was mounted not for luxury,
the boy drowned in the pool for need,
and Sappho fell into the sea.
But to heaven was raped Ganymede.

Jean and I meet among the wrecks
cast by froth and cut from tree
and vanishing in the vortex.
His hair is white prematurely
and I say to him from what I see,
"O poet of the winter sun indeed!"
Who am I is yet to be.
But to heaven was raped Ganymede.

The clawed and wingèd angel, the
Eagle, did not make beauty bleed
bearing him over field and sea,
to heaven was raped Ganymede.

Long Lines

It is not the same to eat candy and to sit down to a dish
      of candy and eat it.
It is not the same to get drunk and to buy a bottle
      in order to get drunk.
I tried to make love in the alley but they wanted
      to go to bed behind locked doors.
I have a bad reputation, they say I have no regard
        for persons
but I have paid fierce attention to each one of
        (hopefully) my simple friends.

In Traffic

All up Eighth Avenue
in his apple-green pie wagon
big Jim and I had a party.
And was that traffic thick
honking us like geese
backed up, I guess, to Wall Street!
while we loitered at a light

and our thoughts were far away.
The looming cop was plenty sore,
"If you'd keep your hands on the wheel
instead of on his prick—" he said,
but Jim unstretched his six-foot-four
and both of them said, "Yeah yeah,"
and we sped away in our cloud
and handily came off
at Columbus Circle.

Swan River

Hardly of the class of rivers, claimed
    on the one side by swamps or water
    fringed by rushes, on the other
among the brooks or freshets to be named

that have a springtime life, Swan River
    is a tiny river of an hour's row,
    forever turning back the prow
like a swan's neck and forever

rounding a bend. Suddenly between
    the willows and the cattails I behold
    Billy dive with a splash. His body is gold,
his penis taut of age thirteen,

his eyes are lapis, his teeth are square,
    and he is laughing. How to get
    to kiss this river boy? His hair is wet
with the dripping moments, he emerges near.

♣

Lloyd (September 9, 1941)

I never, today, went on the court except
to angle sharply tremendous bounces
and catch the young men flat. I'm 30.
But before each play the little Welshman
was stroking in unconscious meditation
his swelling prick, this threw me off my game.
"Hinder!" I said, when my first serve fell short;
my second hit him squarely on the spot,
"Ouch!" says he and lays the offender bare.
"Looks O.K.," say I with expert eyes.
"Yes, ain't it a beauty?" whispers Lloydie.
"I'd better take him home and fix him up"
—and I toss in the ball, to their relief
because today I would have scoured the courts
like Hector when he set the ships afire.
This was the birthday present
that Aesculapius and Eros gave me.
May such an unanimity of joy
reward those who forgo the victory

and leave the courts of glory on an errand
of mercy, and make love instead of war.

Suspicion and Welcome

Fidgeting under my scrutiny
as if he had to pee.
and as if to guard his life
he is opening and closing his jackknife.
Now beware, beware,
stare is grinding against stare.
Then such a smile cerulean spreads
across his frown of doubts and dreads
as when suddenly the breeze
dies and leaves calm seas,
when cries of fisherboy and bird
are ringing in the stillness heard,
and there floats by the *Argo*
with heroes as its cargo.

A Bar in New Orleans

In the amber light and black
    through the cigarette smoke

of the twelve potent faces
     softened to their vices
only Carl was one
     of the original sons
of Genesis, not to be sure
     Adam but the sore
runaways who yet had
     commerce with God
in the old woods, and his crown
     of curly black hair shone.

Three Dirty Poems

Miss Forgetful, how do you do?
I'm pregnant and cannot guess how.
     Let's walk around the block
     and check up on the stock
and deduce a cause or two.

With a tube of grease in his pocket
he walked the avenue to get fuckèd
but every queen in town mistook it
for the hard-on which it lookèd.

The dark armpits of my unwashed
honey taste acrid but her crotch
musky and delicious with
its primrose of the field
where in summer cows browse
in the hollow and bees buzz.
Her tiny lice, seen up close,
wildly wave their legs like spikes
of alfalfa in the gale.

Cold Turkey

A couple of weeks of careless
love and I'm hooked again,
shattered when I can't
score my daily dose.
Sexy, you have doomed me
to cold turkey in Washington,
goose-pimply at the Department
of Health, Education, and Welfare
and biting my nails at Justice.
I thought I was too old to relapse.
You, traitor, are young,

you have lots of fixes,
you aren't in the capital
of the Great Society,
even if your pad is in Brooklyn.

Dolce Stil Nuovo

In Copenhagen one in three
blond or black looks good to me
and since they troop a hundred by
here, give or take a few, are thirty.

And look, how now throughout the Western world
black and blond wear their flowing hair
kempt carelessly almost to the shoulders
—I also ought to write a sweet new style

and call it April. It rains here a lot
but the round sun is rolling in the cloud
silver and is trying to come out
through the great morning fog over Europe.

Sentences

I won't give thee my come
since thee does not regard it
the cream of my hot loins
some silly boy that I
pick up cares more for this
than my royal wife,
I have been spendthrifty
and thee has been ungrateful.

Let George do it let Jim do it
let Tom Dick and Harry do it.
As for me, I'll bawl my nothing
my ancient nothing where
there is no ear to hear.
But midnight is my mother.
I'll write down my complaint
on a yellow end of paper.

For some men fly the mail
between the clouds and the stars
and some are shrewd to garner
the things that money can buy,
I have among the Americans
the gift of honest speech
that says how a thing is
—if I do not, who will do it?

Sex

"Good fun, feeling at peace in the world,
and knowing other people is what sex
has given me, I wish I had more of it.
It makes friends and as if, in so far,
we had a decent city. For the torments
and the super-reality of love
I am too old, I do not need to lose myself,
what I need is health to find myself."
So I explained (God spare me) soberly.
But Eros the physician commented,
"He will have neither health nor love nor sex."

GROWING OLD

"Dreams Are the Royal Road to the Unconscious"

—Freud

The King's Highway to the Dare Not Know,
but I beg my rides and well I know
that boring road where droning hundreds
of cars fade by in hundred-hundreds
of mirror windows all too bright
to see my face, and when the bright
morning breaks I lie like dead.
An old-time surrey, an ancient dead
horse and his farmer stop by the way,
they'll take me one mile on my way
—out of my way—is this the Way?
I used to think I could be happy
but is it possible to be happy?
what is it like? like Plato oh
I'll copy it at large and oh
plan a city where all the distances
—where? whither?—are walking distances.

Boy Scouts

When I was a scout I was our scribe
and that was bully till I lost the books
and quit, I never did become
the patrol leader. But they are plotting
to make me into the scoutmaster.

The patrol leader! he decides
the path to hike in the ferny woods,
he picks the games and chooses up the teams,
and when at night we camp who sleeps with whom
and keeps him company in his pup-tent.

But the scoutmaster, I know his job!
thinks up the trip and buys the tickets
and keeps them out of trouble with the farmer,
frowns at horsing when he has a hard-on himself
and he sleeps with the boy who has the fits.

February 1960

When an irresistible force
meets an immovable object,

stick to it, something has got to give.
Maybe you'll get tired.

A farmer had a horse who wouldn't pull
when he loaded up the wagon,
he just let her stand there for four days,
and she pulled it.

Except another farmer had a horse
that he let stand and she got weak
trying to pull and she fell down
she fell down dead between the shafts.

Such are the pleasing thoughts that fill my mind
on the Pennsylvania railway
in February 1960
going from coast to coast.

An average heart
in a life of seventy years
has exerted so much force
as to lift the largest battleship
fourteen feet out of the water."

Alas, my average heart
has had it, it has had it.
Why do you tax me further,
unresponsive wife?

111

O metal battleship
fourteen feet out of the water,
blaze once with all your guns
before with a terrific
splash you flop back dead
and capsize and sink.

I bore my baby in my arms through the night
like the cantor the Torah dressed in silk
I used as a boy to look at critically.
But his choir sang large chords,
as his figure swung along.
Go to sleep now, daughter, I am old
and very tired carrying you late.
Your father too needs to be comforted.
"I give you good advice," he used to sing,
"do not forsake my law.
She is the tree of life
for those who cleave to her,
her ways are pleasant ways
and all their windings peace."

Sentences

We have a verb "stood up" it means
I kept the date the other didn't,
and damn if once or twice a week
somebody doesn't stand me up.
My verses come back in the mail.
My wife has lied to me.
I am at odds and ends
and walk the streets a maze,

Willie the crazy boy
came to see me yesterday
clowning gaily at
his hilarious ineptitude
to get the slightest satisfaction.
Grandly he proclaimed
"I could renounce the world!"
laughing fit to be tied.

I didn't think when I gave up
my claim to be, my complaint,
and I began to doubt
that I was worthy but neglected,
that I should feel like this
hit-or-miss and happy-go-
unlucky like an Irish pennant
on Somebody's old satchel.

113

When I was trapped, tired and bored,
I sent my shadowself abroad,
      went down the street and boldly had
      the simple joys I was afraid

to take that even easily
the world would have given me,
      and he returned and was glad
      and stood beside where I sat sad.

"Why do you come back?" I said,
"and not abandon me for dead
      with this body that I cannot use?"
      But so it was and so it is.

Among these people I was malcontent,
I gave them what I could and pretty freely
but they could not give me what they had to give
and therefore feared and hurt me, as they could.
To stay my anger, that was issueless,
I didn't see them any more—small loss,
I am sad anyway. So passed a month.

Last night they sent me an ambassador:
what were my grievances? *He* was aggrieved

because I cut them cold; yet it was petty,
he said, to lose for spite without an effort
my friendship rich with profit for them all,
et cetera; he spoke out frank and fair,
passim milking me for new advice,
and *still* he did not give me anything,
not even to respect my malcontent.

Now I am burdened also with his plea
irrelevant to me, yet frank and fair;
he does the best he can, I am to blame.
I profit from it, good! these bitter lines.

Long Lines, 1957

These nights get on my nerves, these sleepless nights.
In the day I can sleep, but what to do with the nights?
Alone, I am not lonely, only I don't fall asleep
—when I was lonely and bitter I could fall asleep.
Out is six flights down, it is another world,
so I sit in bed and write, but hotels in Paris
are cold at 3 A.M. What am I doing here?
"Why, you're writing in your lonely bed just like
        the others."
But I'm not *doing* it, that's just the point.
"Most of the others aren't doing it either."
Ah, then I'm doing it, just like the others.
I wish the pretty Arab who lives in Room 15

would knock and keep me company; I'd knock myself
except he has a friend and they are bound to rob me.
When I think of the long years that I have spent of
     painful nights
and the years of painful days that have been like
     sleepless nights,
I come to no conclusion. Meaning is another world.

In the fussy details
of my overworked life
I am looking for the ticket
I put in the wrong pocket
and for your kind letter
under the heap of trash
the Board of Education
sends me every morning.
I lose my temper quickly
since John went crazy
and you went to Cambridge.
Sometimes I just sit
defeated while a tear
rolls slowly down my cheek.

116

Handball Players

The ball we bought in December
was tired in the shop
and did not want to bounce at all
on the below-freezing court.

Arrogant in their hot
youth the Puerto Ricans
challenged us and smashed the wall.
But Dave and I were cold,

steady and intelligent,
and coldly took their nickels,
dimes and silver quarters
with small shots in the corners.

Oscar Williams

Many of my peers are dying. Daily
I read my friends' doings in the *Times:*
yesterday my brother showed a plan
to the Secretary of the Interior
and Bayard doused a box of dynamite
and kept a boy from blowing up the block.

I see Saul has a play. We are the news
—though it's not the world we wanted to be news in—
and here is Oscar's funny face
peering out from the obituaries.
He wrote to me last week
about a piece of mine on Robert Burns.
I understand it less and less.
My rage is all the more outspoken.
I wish that I had had courage
when I was young and needed it.
But I hadn't yet encountered then
the high and mighty of this earth,
to learn they are like me or Oscar Williams,
or not even.

Perseus

To my dismay as I become
a spokesman in the nation
I have turned into an evil
old man. I do not care about
the young that I make love to
but pay distractedly attention
and talk about my own ideas.
I am too intelligent, I guess,
and well brought up to do much harm
but less and less in love I lash
out at those who make our towns

ugly. Creator Spirit, come.
I think of John who loyally
loved me still while he went mad,
while he went mad and I went sane.
To no one now, never, never,
shall I speak again how it is,
as I used to speak to John,
except to these damned pages
that cannot kiss and come across.
I used to hope because John needed that.
O crazy Hope, where are you lurking lost?
You must be somewhere hiding
for it cannot be I work so hard
just by duty or routine.
No, I have learned to outwit
grisly Disappointment
by working as I look the other way
toward nothing. And loud praise
leaves me also cold.
My name is Perseus. My sword is Simple.
My polished shield is Absence from this world.

＊

"I Thought of the Phrase of Music"

I thought of the phrase of music
    for me to die by
    if it were a play

and it was mine to choose it.
       What friend shall I entrust it to
       to make my deathbed be just so?

But at this grandiose episode
       maybe I have wept
       enough to accept
to die by the wayside
       as I used when I still had
       a penis that grew hard.

That was before I became
       an important man.
       Now my pen has grown
so savage I am ashamed
       and sorry by daylight,
       yet raven again at night.

Lord God who art history
       including the history of me,
       be all this as it may
or any other way
       that chooses me or I choose it
       as I thought of the phrase of music.

     ⚑

Sycamores

My way of showing
       my longing for the Americans

was not to give a damn
        for their morals and opinions.

They have understood me perfectly
        and have made of me a model
for me to keep living up to
        like a statue in the park.

But now I am growing old
        and I am ashamed
of my shabby dress and missing teeth
        and my near-sighted eyes.

And they will have their statue yet
        made of bronze
standing in the sycamores
        whose yellow bark is peeling.

P.W.

Tonight a man passed away
in my house, in my bed.
He rather happily was playing
with my merry daughter
yet he was dead within the hour.
His heart had stopped. Now my own
body is like an enemy
waiting in ambush for me.

I am smoking the tobacco that he left
and picking up the shoes that he left.
Two men are carrying out
the body that he left.
My merry daughter is asleep
in another room.
I must be deep in shock
for it is like a dream.

Long Lines

I opened with my key, to my astonished joy
there in the room stood one I love, for whom I have
longed in my lonely exile, but I said perplexed,
"How did *you* get in?" in an interminable moment
I did not clasp him in my arms, and realized
that he was dead and that this was a ghost.
He said, "When you're dead too we'll be together
as we have failed. I love you, Paul," and was not
and I looked at the key that I was holding in my hand.

April 1966

I see by how the young behave with me
my tired face, my searching eyes

put them off or are grotesque to them.
Yet I persist because my need persists
wooing, sneakily touching
or angrily asking—it is pitiful,
for they seem to like my company
but they avoid being alone with me.
Frustrated I redouble my attempts,
there must be *somebody*, if there are twenty.
My fading mind cannot recall their names.

I am not well. I lie down in distress
to ease my tightening heart. The telephone
rings from Boston, Austin, and Vancouver
colleges inviting me to visit
and be unhappy also there and die.

There it is, and I am quick to say it!
to say again among the Americans
how it is. We poets are like stone.
Give, God, me courage to endure
anyhow, as I have often been
other times in despair and done my work.
Stone is my tried way of being human.

Oh long ago I hoped to be like water
that seeps into low places and lies flat;
blue heaven, a white cloud, and the flock flying north
is the fleeting picture in it
                              —it is springtime
out of my window in California;
happiness would make me healthy here
but the nature of things (and I was a large part)

has in fifty years contrived this trap
in which I lie gasping. Prudently
I wrote thirty books and reared three children
—now it is sprung in April among flowers.

Long Lines: Youth and Age

Like a hot stone your cock weighs on mine, young man,
and your face has become brutish and congested.
I'd stop and gaze at it but drunk with carbon dioxide
we cannot stop snuffling each other's breath.

I am surprised you lust for a grayhead like me
and what a waste for me to grapple so much pleasure
with sliding palms holding your thin body
firmly while you squirm, till it is time to come.

Come, young man . . . I have come with him for company
to his pounding heart. We are wet. Wistfully
I play with his black hair while he falls asleep
minute by minute, slowly, unlike my restless life.

It is quiet on his little boat. "He is a noisy lover,"
I notice idly—the April air is pure—
"but he has no human speech." It's I who say
the words like "I love you" or "Thank you."

HOKKU

Hokku

Blue through the tinted
windshield of the car the wheels
skidding in the storm.

❧

The foundering ship
falls behind and the ship that
sank cannot catch up.

❧

Dusk. Bang the big bell
and drown out the shrill crickets
and shrieking werewolves.

Who in the starshine
where only the gross bulk looms
is it? Ah, it's you.

Hokku for Daisy

    my Now the rainbow
in the falls is growing dim
    the sun clouds over

    and tons of water
my Future vanishes past
    loud and indistinct.

    My little daughter
beside herself is throwing
    sticks in the torrent

    nodding on the edge
a white and yellow daisy
    unwet by the mist.

Do not awaken
the old man might be having
an important dream.

It is a life's work
to swat the flies that get in
through unknown byways

Follies we commit
just to live on a little
turn into money.

Orange and golden
the *New York Times* is blazing
in the village dump.

Hokku for Mathew

Ending of August
still wandering in freedom
    the fens and meadows

    summer in his pail
raspberries and blueberries
    and first blackberries

    three stripes of passage
in my pail as I flounder
    through thorny patches

    sick at heart am I
for my son in the long year
    of the unjust war.

A lighthouse keeper
his portly friends like dreadnoughts
    pass away in night.

Sprayed with strong poison
the roses are crisp this year
in the crystal vase.

With your fists ablaze
with letters and colored stamps
beautiful mailman.

The black shepherd-dog
shook the water off his fur
in a round rainbow.

Hokku for Myself

My seven maples
the branches in silhouette
fading in twilight

my murky old mind
is growing blank for the facts
are impractical

nothing happening
to know in this world I dream
like a wooden post

the moon enlightens
the field and the fieldflowers
with colorless truth.

~✻~

From a high mountain
are visible near and far
many high mountains.

~✻~

Avoid scholarship
in the valley rather farm
and swim in the stream.

❧

Blindly we advance
a thousand suns are falling
one a day westward.

❧

If they were to say
that this hokku was the last
poem that he wrote.

SOME POEMS

Kant

Immanuel Kant that beautiful old man
that character, the most manly and modest
intellect we ever had in the West,
I'd like to taken him to where the Alps
descend in the dark lake in Canton Uri
and watch the terror and the tears of joy
awaken in his knowing eyes. And where
the blue bay of Vesuvius would made
them sparkle and his wrinkles flush with pleasure.
And where, if I could without alarming him,
a teasing pack of pretty Arab hoodlums
hospitably refuse to let him quit
Tunis without a fuck, immensely flustered.
All this I wish I could because I love
that little man who never left Koenigsburg
and well he merited a sabbatical.

Don Larsen's Perfect Game

Everybody went to bat three times
except their pitcher (twice) and his pinch hitter,
but nobody got anything at all.
Don Larsen in the eighth and ninth looked pale
and afterwards he did not want to talk.
This is a fellow who will have bad dreams.
His catcher Berra jumped for joy and hugged him
like a bear, legs and arms, and all the Yankees
crowded around him thick to make him be
not lonely, and in fact in fact in fact
nothing went wrong. But that was yesterday.

The sky was hazy blue, the planes like fish
were pointing up and down the air chalk-white
red and green, it was as gay and bright
a carnival as any child could wish.

I was a rider on the aeroplane
to Cleveland bound on business that I do,
and in that city would I visit too
people I love so much it gives me pain.

We flew so high! three miles above the earth,

the tiny lakes were shining and the streams
meandering reflected the sunbeams.
All added to my wonder and my mirth.

Ajax

Ajax is dead our pet white rat
he died during the night
and Minos his identical twin
in the cage never before alone
will not live very long.

I have brought the body in a box
to throw it in the river
a dirty end for rat or man
but it is still my lordly Hudson
and solemnly I bring the body here.

Two Poems

He slowly beat his feet
until the rhythm locked
the rafters, and the house
rocked from side to side.

Go! go! "Who? me?
what a I done now?"
"You ain't done nuthin,
like you is on fire."

"Call out the fire engingines!"
he pled with knockin knees
and he pissed in his drawers,
was a puddle round his shoes.

Striding Blues

Like a pair o empty shoes
     paddin across the floor
I got the stridin blues
     don' know what for.

Across the hardwood floor
     back an fore, afore an back
all the house is shakin
     like the 1906 earthquake.

Wings sproutin on their heels
     they're crawlin up the wall,
the plaster ceiling has a crack,
     a shoelace is danglin down.

Lines

"Sun-bathing?" No, I lay down in the shade,
now it's too much trouble to move over.
"Oh, you were trying to keep out of the heat,"
he strenuously offered. I said nothing.
"Well, thanks for a good talk," he said briskly
and strolled down to the river where McCoy
was holding his patient line and thoughtfully
playing with himself in the sunshine.
"Catch anything?" our eager friend exclaimed.
The Irishman obligingly spread wide
his legs and fell asleep.
                              Some citizens
are busy producing goods and services,
others of us are not even consumers.

Classics

Suppose *you* would invent a universe,
would you ever strew the Milky Way
or make the mammals fuck and generate
the way they do, so improbably?
On such a scale, in such detail,
it carries you away, how can it fail?

constantly daring. But if you figure
this is a galaxy, the sun a star,
fucking rearranges RNA,
et cetera, et cetera,
it turns out nearly as it is,
this extraordinary production
almost the only world conceivable.
Every classic, Jim, is odd,
stupendous, not altogether sane,
but through and through all of a piece.

Falling Up

The bubbles of gas
speed up in the glass
        just as the sparks
        leap up in the dark.

Nothing is so fair
as this law of t square
        embodied here
        in my glass of beer.

Even more beautiful
is the invisible
        inertia that sinks under
        with inaudible thunder.

New York

Always something new, and now these signs
peremptory green and threatening red
"Walk" "Don't Walk" "Walk" "Don't Walk"
jump up and down like soldiers on the street
City Hall thought it up.
But people circumspectly watch the traffic,
drop a modest eye around the corner,
and flit through a disappearing crevice.

"Circumspect" like crossing Ninth Avenue
"Modest" like asking for a raise
"Nimble" like disregarding bad advice
we walk, if merry were, our merry way.

However, we have unhappy faces
(though human compared with the Americans),
for my native city has become worn and dirty
like an old shoe that doesn't even fit.

A Review at Watkins Glen

Trim squadrons oiled and lit by beer
the Central New York Volunteer

Firemen come marching by
from Seneca to the Fairgrounds.

Here is something rarely seen,
Tioga has an engine green!
    hurrah for that bold emerald
    aglow, four hats on either rack,

my vote goes to Tioga. And
Horseheads has the loudest band.
    And Hector and Ovid and Virgil
    do not discredit their namesakes.

They climb up ladders into space
and haul the hose with speed and grace
    astounding, drunken as they are
    beside the sparkling water.

The Siege
—Aristotle, *Politics*, II, 7

To ferret Eubulus out of his nest
for honor, justice, and the rest,
Autophradatus came in panoply
horse and ship, land and sea.
Atarne-town prepared for death,
armed in turn and held its breath.

At twilight came a messenger
to the besieger to confer.
"How much will this siege cost,
the armor and the engines lost,
the rations and the daily pay?
Make up an itemized account
and for sixty percent of the amount
Eubulus will go away."

Autophradatus with a frown
—bad at figures—marked it down,
whistled, had the bugles blown,
and left at the crack of dawn.

"Now what can you say?"
cackled the septuagenarian,
"I've proved it can be done!
Not in jail, nor in disgrace,
I did not die by violence
nor ruin myself as you predicted.
Victory! victory!"
—So cried the king of beasts
in his social cage
and the angelic choir
covered their heads with their wings.

The Bone

With narrow eyes, sucking on my long pipe,
I see the time is over-ripe
to change the animal I am
from dog, who's friend to man, to be a man.
My tail will no longer thump the floor
and I will not wait hungry at the door.
I used to like to sniff at Lassie and Lad
and try to mount them, but a dog is sad.

Our zoo is rich with the wild and tame
totems that we devoured and became.
Perry's a moose: moose are misunderstood,
they stand the spread-horned monarchs of the wood
until the hunter fires and they fall dead
and their horns above the mantel spread.
My Gene's a monkey who flies up a tree
and pisses on the passers by with glee,
but George is a brown bear rough and surly
who oughtn't to get out of bed so early.
Glenn, a stallion whose nostrils flare
shies away skittish as a yearling mare.
Sally's a kangaroo, her one word *Ouch!*
she vehemently jumps, but in her pouch
she guards a secret that she will release
one day in the land-cut-off Antipodes.
Fritz, who's an elephant, says every hussy
would be a panther or other glorified pussy,

and that pussy of his pounces on the harp
and like her claws the melody is sharp.
My little boy, I guess, is a wild-jackass
who hee-haws as he kicks me in the face
—all amiable animals!
                              This middle-size
spotted mongrel, jaunty with enterprise,
has barked his bark. But now the man
must choose what beast to be, for he can.
Look in the glass: I do not like him much,
the man, I am not used to being such.
What would it be like to be like that?
He doesn't show the horror in my heart
but maybe the impatience—his lips are taut—
he seems to say, "Dog, finish! there's no use
to worry the bone once you have the juice."

                    ☧

He got arrested because he was lonely
and they have put him into solitary.

He went mad to be like everybody
and they have made him mayor.

                    ☧

Can one straight forward march and bawl and bawl?
See, can one not!

The Past

Every gain has its loss, not every loss
    its gain but sinks into the waste
the primal pain unplastic the chaos
    without a future the astounding past

O monument of agony! if I could
    carve you a few hacking strokes
unfinished, you'd be worthy to be stood
    in Florence among the other rocks.

Moses
—*Pensées*, viii, 458

On the yeasty water the wild torrent
of vice, of need, despair, disgrace,
to death, to death, the jaws of death

little Moses in a bowl
sits dry of flesh and sure of soul
through it all

—to whom the Princess from behind
her stylish linen hood will smile
and he shall stand within the Porch
of Heavenly Jerusalem.

Wellfleet Harbor Wind Sun Space

North Wind across the dunes and bays,
sweep away hatred, be praise.
    Hatred has been half of me
    but it's boring, praise is free.

Hot Sun, who makes earth green and tan,
give heat and color to this man.
    The blank morose where I have been
    is dull, I long for tan and green.

Great Spaces of the bays and islands
and ocean crashing down from the horizon,
    without effort here you are,
    make me be here who have been far.

I am a native, on my home
rocks of the world I play like foam,
    my quick spirit gives delight
    and little children send me soaring like a kite.

The day was clear as day
March like the start of spring
everywhere the sky
spread wider than the earth

the clouds were shapes of vapor
in the high atmosphere
the light came from the sun
the heat of it was warm

the clouds rested secure
at the height they were,
just this density
choosing just this pressure.

that past day was
it is written down in words
how my only world
went with me as I walked.

SENTENCES AND PRAYERS

Sentences for Mathew Ready

1. Agree to give it up
    and do yourself without:
    of course a world-for-you is lost
    but you can't cope anyway;
    likely another world
    will come to be and be exciting,
    though you can't *know;* this you believe,
    why don't you act accordingly?

2. People tend to like me who know me
    nor am I shy to pick up friends,
    that I am usually unhappy
    is only mathematical,
    rarely is anyone both lovely and available;
    I am aggressive, modest, and cowardly,
    a congeries not doomed to prosper,
    but pious and grateful unto thee, O Luck.

3. Because the good die young
    and the wages of sin is death
    I steer a middle course,
    alive to tell the tale;
    so have I and my world

matured on speaking terms,
measuring from time to time
each other with a glance.

4. This sequoia is three thousand years old,
    fires and lightning, drouth and earthquakes
    have been the drama of its world;
    millennia ago it overtopped
    the competition of the undergrowth;
    only in this decade is it threatened
    by the feet of our hordes trampling the roots
    who come by here to gaze at age with awe.

5. Whoever the soldier was who stole
    these Vaphio cups, he was a judge of gold
    better than soldiers I have met,
    maybe he was a farmer who knew bulls
    entangled in the ropes. We others but
    who have no gods or burial deposits
    wander from Eleusis to Delphi
    gathering meanings that do not add up.

6. Will it occur to me? and when will it occur?
    the imprecise answer to a question
    I never learned rightly to formulate.
    I listen to sentences of Mozart
    that gracious condescending spirit,
    but there is no answer here for me,
    I did not have a lucky father,
    I did not rebel just when.

7. Lying on your back in the meadow
    the finer resolution of a cloud
    is worth little and blue sky
    is bluer without lenses,
    take your glasses off;
    best is to drowse and see
    sharply another dream
    than this familiar nightmare.

8. An eagle on a rock
    lighting with wings upreared
    and in his beak a writhing snake,
    such are my liberties:
    freedom of the spirit
    long since corrupted me
    into an indignant
    citizen who cannot sleep.

9. Let me praise rapid speech
    that says how a thing is,
    in my dear English tongue
    that I learned from a child
    forty years and more
    carefully I have copied
    the meters of my breathing
    and pruned out thoughts not mine.

10. One is running away
    one is running after
    one is running dreaming
    of the Olympic games
    —across the lush lawn

enclosed by eucalyptus—
one is just running
and him my eyes follow.

11. Last night the moon came close:
what was picture has become
shore where men will land.
Astronomers and engineers
wide-eyed on steppe and beach
mount their guns and fire
fraught with future, acting
in single-minded darkness.

12. The earth and sky so carried on this month
as if the poor earth never could recover,
whipped by hurricanes and drowned by floods
and stung all night by lightning,
were her lurid jewels. Some are dead,
the newspapers are rich with marvelous
and pathetic pictures and reports.
This morning she has on her sunny clothes.

13. I let the ball bound by
to field the sun appearing
out of the blue storm-cloud
silvery and pouring
light, light—oh how
how to get out of this
fool baseball game that I
no longer want to play?

14. He had five sons, Reaper and Thresher,
    Mechanic, Wayward, and Daring,
    they were his pride and easy to praise
    (like himself). He was ingenuous
    and did not see how people envied him,
    and they were glad he fell into misfortune
    and that his beautiful boys hung their heads
    in the bitter world where they walked.

15. Like the drowsy child who can't untie
    his knotted shoelace, he is cross,
    why doesn't he fall over
    and slide to sleep with one shoe on
    like Willy Winkle my son John?
    —my presence is noticeable to few
    and good and necessary to nobody,
    why bother? what matter?

16. I know it was
    but I can't find anywhere
    that photo of my face
    age of eleven
    with a gappy grin
    and eyes frankly leering
    out of what window
    looking at what ocean?

17. Daybreak I look into the cloudy sky
    for a telegram from the Messiah

and disappointed sit in bed all day
brooding about the Way.
Impatiently I listen for the knock
that didn't happen fifty years ago
and devise for the advantage of you all
vengeful reforms, some of them practical.

18. What a lousy parliamentarian!
     forced on a minor issue to a show of strength:
     I lost to the coalition, my allies
     mumbled in the voice vote, I demanded
     a roll call, but they stayed in the lobby;
     even now I can't believe it,
     I was steam-rollered, there is some mistake,
     it never even came to a showdown.

19. They closed my bar, revoked the license,
     and Teddy, Bobby Edmonds, and Bill Brown
     and other harmless hustlers and mad queens
     are scattered up and down Eighth Avenue.
     They were a bore—it was a lousy bar—
     but it was ours; they gave me tips
     that kept me out of trouble up to now,
     now here I stand, staring at a padlock.

20. In error, incompetent,
     I failed to stop (perhaps I sped)
     his onward wreck:
     wild as his wits were, mine were blank;
     he screamed for help and my marrow froze;
     I could not quit him without hurting him

nor, if I remained, come across.
In error, incompetent.

21.   A grounder to short and out at first
      is our sharp fate. We are not heavy hitters.
      The reapers grin at us across the infield.
      I was powerless to help my friend,
      I shall be powerless to help myself.
      We two were lovers, but the field we played
      did not look like this world—the grass was ragged,
      the players shouted out encouragement.

22.   My head is low with my horrible luck
      my icy eyes staring starkly
      hasty and wholly hand and hoping
      I freely offered, it was not enough
      men doubted I meant it. But it doesn't matter
      for my strength is slight my will too weak
      to win anyway even though earnest
      so my world is waste. But my work is well.

23.   When I was a child, my mother threatened
      to abandon me, or did. But my world
      my only one never made that threat;
      although she was a wall she was there
      even when I whimpered for my earache
      and screamed for what I needed and couldn't have.
      Lately, however, I have fallen ill
      and my only world is making that old threat.

24.   Oh yes, I'd write more poetry
      about my little daughter Daisy

except she is so live and sweet
and pretty that she doesn't fit
the black mood and painful breath
of my present thoughts about death
and the sarcasm of my
present thoughts about my country.

25. Woeful was the winter
my politics proved futile,
despite me John went mad,
and my sister started to die;
nevertheless, though tattered
in my self-esteem,
I deserve to have survived
to this bright Tuesday.

26. Gun-metal the earth below
shark's-belly the horizon round
I wing from where he punched his fist
through glass and poured in pints
his chemical-contaminated blood
ruby on the pavement—gladly
South! away from where his cold
speeches made my hair turn gray.

27. In this cloud it is confused
though above the cloud clear and bright.
It chooses me to stay confused

in this cloud in gusts of wet
among erratic slow long bolts
of lightning and I am afraid
of falling down. It is not blue
and rose and pearl where I fly.

28.   The engingines
of the ailingplane
are stuttering
I hope they won't
beginnnn
to stammer:
30,000 feet
is too high for speech defects

29.   Out of sight of my lover I soon became frightened,
much was unfinished, I never had had
enough in the hurried conditions I managed,
on my lonely voyage I worried over
an unlikely danger I foresaw in flashes,
I reread for safety something I wrote
busying myself making small corrections,
and I wrote something new to ward off the unknown.

30.   Most ancient dreams and fables
are poorly realized
but this great aeroplane
is very like the Roc
and so softly descends
with clumsy grace and lands us
alas in New York City
nor am I Sindbad.

31. You ask what is the bay with the statue
    down there and the new bridge across the Narrows:
    I call it "Splendid." And Manhattan's phalanx
    of warrior skyscrapers on the right,
    I call it "Towering." But these fleecy clouds
    are "Sweet" our plane is slowly nosing into
    the blueness as we leave the haze behind
    at nine, according to the pilot, thousand feet.

                        ❧

32. "Forward cars for Baltimore and Washington,
    B. and W. all the way up ahead!"
    they really have impressed that message on me
    but no one offers to tote my heavy heart
    leaving behind my home where Daisy is
    learning to speak and she cries "Cow! cow!"
    also when it's a horse. The Capitol,
    though it is white, will not shine as sunny.

33. God damn! a hundred people on a train,
    not one worth groping. What do you do
    for four hours? "Sit quiet in your seat
    and twiddle your thumbs like everybody else,
    studiously read the *New York Times*."
    Is that what others do? I don't believe it.
    I look and so it is: I am dumbfounded.
    —This keeps me occupied as far as Trenton.

34. There's never a sexy youth
    on the train to Washington
    nor do the elder statesmen
    have humane wrinkles and good eyes;
    sometimes I meet a foreign scholar
    and we speak each other's language badly,
    as wearily I return
    to my little flat under the Capitol.

35. The sunrise and a warm sailor
    made waiting worthwhile,
    it was only looks averted quick
    and lots of fright was in his eyes
    but his prick swelled and so did mine
    and thank God for a sign of life
    in January, 8 A.M.
    at Dulles International Airport.

36. Riding to Washington on a mission congenial
    to my nature, to be a disinterested judge,
    I am well pleased with me today and rapidly
    sketching a little book important for the nation:
    every hour flashes in my mind the soon
    scene when I shall have come away at last
    to my pretty farm on the Connecticut
    and you arriving on your motorcycle.

37. I am looking forward to going away
    and how far shall I go?
    to my pretty home in New Hampshire
    where trout leap in the ragged river?
    to prison where the powers that be
    will pen me up to hush my voice?

or shall I drift as far as death
like into fog on the Grand Banks?

38. The wheel Charles left me, that I christened
     "Johnny Wells," and Charles' ghost knows why,
     I do not keep so scrupulous as he
     used to keep everything except his life;
     and yet our Johnny still outstrips
     lesser wheels on the dusty road,
     though I do not ride so tirelessly far
     as Charlie used to do, before he died.

⁂

39. All day along the shore to Alpine
     they have been line-fishing and trapping crabs,
     I hunting cock, that's an unlicensed sport.
     The dusk is dull and few of us have any
     game to boast, except the afternoon
     and the endless largo of the flood
     and the sun with his hairs on end in fright
     as down he sinks behind the Palisades.

40. "O Devil who find work
     for idle hands, find me
     something, for I am jobless
     to grind my teeth and spit out porcelain."
     So carelessly I prayed,
     and out of the bureau of Hell

called "Work for Idle Hands"
they sent me you to grope.

41. You said my lust was like the insistent
     mosquitoes in the barn-loft where we slept,
     this broke my heart—do you know?—
     because I loved you very much
     and you found a telling metaphor,
     I could not remedy that fault
     not since my bleak childhood
     unsure, abandoned, hungry.

42. After I'd stared awhile, I heard a voice:
     "I see that your primeval dream,
     your Easter Island face,
     has come to dainty lines
     —you like your soup weak," Eros jeered,
     "your punch is weak too, nothing comes
          from nothing."
     I turned and there the face of horror was,
     but I at this one also idly stared.

43. If he grinds his back teeth like a paranoic
     that's one thing, but if he is swallowing
     and his trouser's fly begins to bulge
     that's quite another; some play with a knife
     and some make a fist to warn you off.
     Others feign sleep and languorously stretch
     their lanky legs out long and lick their lips;
     but I, if I feign sleep, fall asleep.

44. Lovely in the distance
    are dull at the approach,
    but you were like a doll
    and loomed like heaven near;
    your hair was chocolate
    your deep blue eyes were frank
    and you were taken by
    the rapture on my face.

45. I wish we could already fly
    to the moon or another planet
    lesser of gravity so you and I
    could make love unencumbered by
    our heavy bodies. Weight is sweet
    but it's sweeter to hold you close light,
    not—God forbid—that I'm complaining
    of what we have, very good.

46. I wrote a long and simple play that moved
    a few to tears, so slowly it unwound,
    like Bruckner's music, but most people found
    nothing in my play of interest.
    But in the other room this afternoon
    Baylis played the Symphony of Spring
    just for me, to say something to me,
    and he is like a slowly bounding deer.

47. His beauty sparkles, his big eyes blaze,
    his moist teeth gleam and his wide smile
    turns up a lamp that was aglow,
    his laughing-wrinkles crackle like a campfire;
    the flush across his neck

is like the slowly burning ruby
I drowned in swimming for tomorrow
west into the blushing sea.

48.　Given six or seven
the beauty of them likes me, beauty's kind.
The rest don't see it and get angry
with their tight mouths and squinty eyes,
unmagnanimous animals.
The face that has the golden glow
smiles me welcome. People say otherwise,
but lust is the magnet of beauty.

49.　Waxing and waning with the seasons, fifty years
I've walked this ten-thousand-mile trail
along the shore to here, that's a long hike.
No wonder I plod heavily along
and climb the rocky spots unsteadily.
Yet never till June 1961
have I studied with such winter-starved eyes
the rhododendron thick on this cliffside.

50.　Of things I use and that use me
you my modest old black car
cause me little cursing
unlike my wife or son or dog
or soul or body. I have often marveled
how you have started at a touch

climbed the hill picking up speed
and gently taxied into Groveton.

51.   From first base on the left
on a clockwise diamond
he threw me toward home plate
a pure white bounding ball
I did not field, for heaven
above his ebony head
broke through the curtain cloud
silver: I saw it all.

52.   With drooping groping toes
and black tips of bobbing bills
the gulls touch the water
and hover in the wind and scream,
a game—no one catches a fish—
or an obsession—touch and go—
high a thousand yards
they soar into the silent sky.

53.   "Man, I'm shook to see you in a commercial,
I thought you was opposed to advertising."
This is news-casting, damn it, these *are* good,
National Biscuit's *Triscuits*—crunch crunch—
not so good as nooky or Vivaldi
but—crunch crunch—better than Ingmar Bergman
or the academic friends that I—crunch crunch
crunch crunch—ever made in Milwaukee.

54.   Now only praise makes me cry,
when David Hume praises Alfred

I read it through a shine of tears,
and if a poet praises loud
—naturally loud is praise—an ancient
hero who never lived in this world,
then my heart breaks and I bawl
for joy in this land of loss.

55. Aligned at last the bass-drummer
picked up his drum and the leader
twirled his baton and forward all
they stepped and big the brasses blared.
My heart leaped up, I laughed for joy,
because I am the Muses' boy
and never people are so fair
as making music loud and clear.

56. I have outlived last winter!
April! I am not dead!
the ancient exclamation
of Eleusis. Dead do not
cry out anything nor bring
sheaves to Demeter.
The dead did not outlive last winter
but I have outlived last winter.

57. "Great Tao is a ship adrift"—awakes
at sunrise asking, where am I?
and deviates forward slowly to nowhere.
What does he know? to front afraid the gale
and painfully climb the next oncoming wave.
It is by an inevitable mistake

that the ten thousand cheer and shake their flags
lining the shore in the indifferent port.

58. Though little of what I try succeeds,
most of what I try has meaning.
God keeps after me
in his pedagogic way.
I was accepted long ago
into this university,
listen to my tone of voice
and you will know an upper-classman.

Little Prayers

1. God, do you make me happier,
for by my doing I am here
    and the outlook is even worse
    as I grow old. I have been cautious

not prudent, and unusually thoughtful
not wise. But indefatigable
    has been my love whether I could
    or not, which you count highly, God.

2. Dull, miserable, and ailing
my way of life to which I clung
    stubbornly and often I
    disapproving proved my way

cannot work, it is not viable,
I am foredoomed to terrible
    years I cannot remedy.
    Life-saver, rescue me.

3. I never did, Lord, believe
that me you have preserved alive
    for any remarkable day
    or use—much as my country

needs brains and bravery.
But to be staring stupidly!
    to be drifting toward disgrace!
    to call for help too spiritless!

4. Stop keeping the home-things alive,
my balky body, their grudging love,
    so forth: let them die if they want.
    I grew this avocado plant

that never throve and survives skinny
—it has ceased to be a symbol for me,
    Let it dry! And yet I pour
    for pity's sake this glass of water.

5. Whether I am close to death
or not, God of Breath,
    I do not know, nor what,
    dark God, to do with that.

But my palms are wet and cold
and a pure fear has taken hold

of my heart. This I know,
O simple God and true.

6. Lost—God help me—in a waste
where the dusk has fallen fast
　　I panic and my cowardice
　　is what it always was.

　　No light, no guide, but now thank God
　　my wet tears are welling hot
　　　　and I can breathe in the black night
　　　　and look about as I wait.

7. Fear with me walks abroad and where
I live I am afraid. I am aware
　　of many real dangers. Others
　　are imaginary fears.

　　Yet I seek, neither, Lord, your peace
　　nor the momentary happiness
　　　　that I used to seek to ward
　　　　off terror, Lord.

8. I have thought of my aunt singing
when I was a child the air of Puccini,
　　she is long dead who vividly
　　returns to me in a memory

　　and I, O Lord, shall be dead
　　like her: is it this certitude

that has destroyed my hope and joy
and when I see beautiful things I cry?

9. The flashing summer we forecast,
the bright beach, the dark forest,
    and to tour the famous sights
    of Europe, prospects of delight

—but Lord, our name is Joyless, we have
dry voices and our looks are heavy.
    Rescue us, we are immersed
    in the sin of waste, which is the worst.

10. By murder and arrest
my frantic night is tossed,
    awaking I look forward
    either to peace, Lord,

or doom, in doubt which,
bound home from far And such
    is my travel prayer
    to the Savior.

11. As if my purpose was to drown
the shining ship I did abandon
    that was not sinking, rapidly
    she stood away, I did not try

to swim, yet was about to cry
help when I awoke and thereby
    helped myself, though I was wistful
    of the depths of the whirlpool.

12. Surceaser of foreboding! I gave up
    myself to you to shatter and reshape
        in the plastic order of your world,
        stranger than the world controlled

    by my rage. And you have bade
    me lay my plans in solitude
        with what initiative I can
        muster when my heart is broken.

13. God, I prayed, to me restore
    some kind of thing to hope for
        that, only, creates energy
        from nothing for another day,

    but You instead have sent Your angel
    Indignation with his bugle
        to waken the Americans at midnight.
        Give me health and I will fight.

14. Not on our knees do we
    ask but hear our plea,
        Author of liberty.
        America our country

    has been leased out. We must and will
    reclaim her at our own peril,
        but do You faithfully ignite
        on the hilltop freedom's light.

15. Creator spirit, please let your
    soft lamp the soul of our poor

land illumine and its am-
ber comfort us. I am

familiar with your grace when you
call me to look out the window
　　and quiet with its stars is heaven
　　and men are doing what they can.

16.　If I undertake to be
　　the conscience of my country,
　　　　I do, Lord, do my duty.
　　　　But, Lord, it was not I

　　who chose it, but the hungry heart
　　and level look that you allotted
　　　　to me when you did burden
　　　　with different gifts different men.

17.　God bless this small home that
　　I by habit decorate;
　　　　avert the fire, fill the space
　　　　if not by joy at least by use;

　　make my daughter safe from the pest
　　and my wife bear if that be best
　　　　and many friends for many years
　　　　learn to climb our steep stairs.

18.　I do not much collaborate
　　not out of spite, but they are not
　　　　my peers, I disregard
　　　　their claims. It is too bad.

But God He is my master and
apprentice I wait His command.
    He asks me what I think of it
    and Him I tell my best thought.

19. I talk to you because I have no one
else, the two or three are gone
    to whom I told my murky thought
    because they cared for that.

I said thanks to them, Lord, also
more than I ever do to you:
    you are as close to my touch
    but I do not know your love as much.

20. I waited in the parlor, Lord,
in panic for the messenger Your word
    for whom I had, as both we knew,
    no answer or excuse. But You,

You, as often, Lord! had stolen
through the back door into the kitchen
    and seated at the table quietly
    were pouring coffee for Yourself and me.

Four Little Prayers

21. My island by another week
    has drifted like a rusty wreck
        without a steersman. From the beach
        with hopeless eyes I watch

    her go. I would swim out
    to her but you have also put
        chains on my ankles. What,
        Father, do You mean by that?

22. Yes, weariness and grief
    is a fair description of my life
        —I wonder if
        others are better off.

    I have also written,
    like now, these facts down
        and this has given me
        pride if not much joy.

23. How wistfully I envy
    without hostility
        the young who race and breathe
        without thinking of death.

    I used to try to know them
    and made advances to them

who now seem like a different
species in the environment.

24. In a panic and compelled
as when once a devil held
the knife to my heart and I
had no choice but to obey,

I was a child, I could not run away,
my palms were cold and wet. Today
but, Father of fugitives, I am old
though my palms are wet and cold.

Index of First Lines

Dragging its feet the spring, 88
Dull, miserable, and ailing, 170
Dusk. Bang the big bell, 127

Ending of August, 130
Every gain has its loss, not every loss, 148
Everybody went to bat three times, 138

Fear with me walks abroad and where, 172
Fidgeting under my scrutiny, 100
First through blooming fields of hell among, 38
Follies we commit, 129
For God's sake, sailor, I'd be glad, 93
"Forward cars for Baltimore and Washington, 162
For wearing out the spirit with dull size, 37
From a high mountain, 132
From first base on the left, 168

Garnered in twenty books, 12
Gene, John, Jojoy, Jerry, 86
Given six or seven, 167
God bless this small home that, 175
God damn! a hundred people on a train, 162
God, do you make me happier, 170
God, I prayed, to me restore, 174
Good fun, feeling at peace in the world, 105
"Great Tao is a ship adrift"—awakes, 169
Gun-metal the earth below, 160

Hardly of the class of rivers, claimed, 98
He got arrested because he was lonely, 147
He had five sons, Reaper and Thresher, 157
He's drunk again and doesn't show, 94
He slowly beat his feet, 139
He was a beautiful mechanic, 73
His beauty sparkles, his big eyes blaze, 166

183

Paul Goodman, a native New Yorker, was born in 1911. After graduating from City College in New York, he received his Ph.D. in humanities from the University of Chicago. Mr. Goodman has taught at the University of Chicago, New York University, Black Mountain College, Sarah Lawrence, the University of Wisconsin, and has lectured widely at various universities throughout the country. He is associated with the New York and Cleveland institutes for Gestalt Therapy and the University Seminar on the City at Columbia. He is also a Fellow of the Institute for Policy Studies in Washington, D.C.

Mr. Goodman has written for *Commentary*, *Politics*, *Kenyon Review*, *Resistance*, *Liberation*, *Partisan Review*, etc. His fiction includes *The Facts of Life*, *The Break-Up of Our Camp*, *Parents' Day*, *The Empire City*, and *Making Do*, as well as *The Young Disciple*, *Faustina*, *Jonah: Three Plays*. *Kafka's Prayer* and *The Structure of Literature* are books of criticism. In the area of social studies, in addition to being the co-author of *Communitas* (available in Vintage Books) and *Gestalt Therapy*, he has written *Like a Conquered Province: The Moral Ambiguity of America*, *Art and Social Nature*, *People or Personnel: Decentralizing and the Mixed System*, *Drawing the Line* (a pamphlet); and (available in Vintage Books) *Growing Up Absurd*, *Utopian Essays and Practical Proposals*, *Compulsory Mis-education*, and *The Community of Scholars*.

In addition to *Hawkweed*, Mr. Goodman has published a volume of verse entitled *The Lordly Hudson*.

Mr. Goodman is married and has three children.